You Taught My Feet To Dance

Learning to Follow His Lead

ERICA MARIE FOSTER

Unless noted, all Bible quotations are from the the Amplified® Bible, copyright © 1954, 1958, 1962, 1964, 1965, 1987 by The Lockman Foundation. Used by permission. (www.Lockman.org)

Scripture quotations marked NASB are from the New American Standard Bible®, Copyright © 1960, 1962, 1963, 1968, 1971, 1972, 1973, 1975, 1977, 1995 by The Lockman Foundation.

Scripture quotations marked NIV are taken from the Holy Bible, New International Version®, NIV®. Copyright © 1973, 1978, 1984, 2011 by Biblica, Inc.™ All rights reserved worldwide. www.zondervan.com. The "NIV" and "New International Version" are trademarks registered in the United States Patent and Trademark Office by Biblica, Inc.™

Scripture quotations marked NKJV are from the New King James Version®. © 1982 by Thomas Nelson. All rights reserved.

Printed in the United States of America
2016 First Edition

Subject Index:
Foster, Erica Marie
Title: You Taught My Feet To Dance: Learning to Follow *His* Lead
1. Christian 2. Inspirational 3. Parenting 4. Family Relationships

Paperback ISBN: 978-1-943526-57-4
Hardback ISBN: 978-1-943526-56-7
LCCN: 2016910506

Author Academy Elite, Powell OH

To protect the privacy of the individuals, some names have been changed.

ENDORSEMENTS

"This book is the life experience of a young woman who loves God and has a desire to know Him even to the point of fellowshipping in His suffering. Through her story you will come to know that even when followers of Jesus endeavor to serve God with all of their hearts, people, events, and circumstances can impact their longing to perfectly serve Him.

You will see Erica Foster grieve over the death of the vision she believed was God's for her and her children. You will see her come to grips with that death and watch as God healed her personal hurts and provided new purpose and meaning. As you read the story of this journey, you will see God at work behind the scenes being Jehovah Jireh, our provider. For those who have walked a similar path, the life of Erica will give you hope and someone with whom you can identify. For all of us there is cause here to rejoice in the sustaining goodness of our God.

As Erica's pastor the last five years leading up to the writing of this book, I have been privileged to watch the body of Christ be the New Testament church. They have gathered around Erica and poured the love of Jesus on her and her children.

Her story is not yet complete, and I watch with anticipation and expectancy to see what the Lord has in store in the chapters yet to come.

Be blessed as you read!"

Pastor Dave Gross
Radiant Life Church
Dublin, Ohio

"Erica Marie Foster - I sensed the presence of God the moment she was laid in my arms. Erica has always been shy, quiet, strong willed and compassionate. After giving her heart to Jesus at a young age, her favorite chapter in the Bible became John 15 (the fruit of the vine). Her greatest desire from the time she was little was to become a wife and mother. Even though Erica has suffered great heartache and the death of her dream, God has proven to Erica that He is our very present help in the time of need and He is the restorer of her family. Erica's dad and I stood by all of her life watching her develop into a kind, gentle, giving, loving mother and daughter. Erica has a teachable spirit and wants to glorify God in everything she says and does. I can honestly say that she is walking a life of unending forgiveness and grace towards her situation and toward her former husband. She is truly dancing upon all her disappointments. I thank God for the honor and privilege of being her mom."

Carol Esther Myers (Erica's Mom)

"I met Erica over 20 years ago, just after she & her husband were married. Although they moved to Florida about a year after we met, Erica & I stayed in touch via lengthy phone calls & visits here & there. I have had the honor of "Rejoicing" with Erica through the years over the birth of her 5 beautiful blessing's & witnessing the providential hand of God on her life by continually providing for she & her children. I have also shared in "Weeping" with Erica over the loss of her precious earthly Father & the grieving over a husband who abandoned her & her children. Erica (to me) is an amazing testimony of a Woman of Grace. I am honored to call her "Sister in Christ" & friend."

Deena Laubenthal
(Homeschooling Wife and Mother of Five)

"I am overjoyed that Erica is sharing with us her story of hardship, oppression, and yet unwavering, unending, and unstoppable faith in her Lord and Savior Jesus Christ. She is a dedicated mother of five children whose selflessness, integrity and excellent character have proven themselves over and over again throughout her story. You will find encouragement and the knowledge that God will never leave you or forsake you throughout the pages of this book. It will empower you to keep on striving for a deeper relationship with Christ no matter what you are going though."

Craig and Heather Bjerke
(Servants of Christ and parents of five)

"I have had the privilege and honor of knowing Erica for over 30 years. She has been a friend and mentor to me - someone I look up to and want to be like. I have seen her walk through some of life's most difficult valleys and watched her remain steadfast and act with integrity. Erica is a loving mother who teaches her children both through her words and by her actions. She is a beautiful woman, both inside and out, and her story is a testimony of the Lord's provision and grace and is truly an inspiration."

Shelley Noel
(Long Time Friend)

"God is faithful even when man is not. Erica's life is a living testimony of God's goodness and love. The scripture states, "I have never seen the righteous forsaken or His seed begging for bread." (Ps.37:25) I have known Erica for 15 years and time after time I have sat back amazed at the Lord's provision for her family. He is the God who gives Hope to the hopeless, brings Peace to the broken-hearted and fills our lives with Joy! It is evident by the joy on her and her children's faces that He has been a faithful and loving Heavenly Father. Although they have walked through many trials, intense hardship and deep pain, her and her kids know that He is their Father and their Friend. This book is powerful and life changing. I couldn't stop reading it."

Gina Granville
(Longtime friend and Homeschooling mother of 4)

"I was honored to be one of Erica's readers before she published her book and I have to say, apart from the Bible, I've not read a book I enjoyed so much and I actually know the author! The book draws you into His presence and you begin to worship God."

Nancy Sofowora
(Friend and fellow church member)

This Book is dedicated to my five children:
Weston Cole
Adelynn Grace
Dalton Chase
Audrynn Esther
Azaliah Hope

To know you is to love you. Each one of you has made such a difference in my life. You are my inspiration. I love you from the bottom of my heart and thank God daily for the privilege and honor of being your mom.

Learn to worship with your wounds,

Praise with your problems,

Move with your mess,

Sing through the sorrow,

And **DANCE** in the drought!

-Rev. Samuel Rodriguez

CONTENTS

FOREWORD

An individual like Erica is rare—someone who is unaware of the power of her own story. Such is often the case when we doubt our own significance. We wonder if our lives matter enough to be shared in a way that will help others through their own pain. I remember interviewing Erica about the potential of becoming one of our authors. I saw a unique spark, and I heard a riveting story. But I didn't know if she believed in herself enough to invest the time and resources in her dream. However, as she clung to her Creator for strength, Erica chose the hard road, believed in herself, and decided to invest in her dream. Sure it was a tough process. I saw her go through times of doubt and frustration. But as she persevered, faced her biggest fears, and boldly started writing, she was transformed into a courageous version of herself.

Erica did the deep internal work, bravely confronted her past, and as a result embraced a powerful new future. I am utterly convinced that God will use her story in a mighty way. Get ready to experience real, gut honest, powerful stories of how God taught Erica how to dance upon life's pain, disappointments, and failures.

I am proud of Erica and honored God used me to be her coach and servant leader.

Kary Oberbrunner, CEO of Igniting Souls. Co-creator of Author Academy Elite. Author of *ELIXIR Project, Day Job to Dream Job, The Deeper Path,* and *Your Secret Name.*

INTRODUCTION

If your joy is hindered because of your intense pain or if you have been abused and abandoned, rejected and have suffered from great loss and loneliness, I encourage you to read this book. This is the true story of the last 10 years of my life. I bravely share my journey because I want you to know that I understand how it feels to be utterly alone even when you have people surrounding you, how it feels to have such extreme pain you want something or someone to take the pain away and how it feels to be completely overwhelmed with life you don't even know how to function. However, through it all God taught and is still teaching me in the most unexplainable ways how to *dance* upon all my pain and disappointments. He has taught me to live my life along with my five children with faith, freedom, purity, and hope.

During this time of intense writing I tried to quit many times. It took me over six months just to write the first few chapters. I wrote them and rewrote them many times, asking God to give me the right words. It was extremely difficult to be so vulnerable and to write anything negative about my former marriage. For years I tried to cover up my story and pretend it never happened, until my fourteen year old daughter Adelynn, wrote a poem about the scar she has on her chin. It brought me to tears and ministered to me in such a profound way.

When she was two years old, she fell, and her face hit the corner of a shelf. She ended up having to get eight stitches. Since then, people have constantly asked her what happened to her face. I have asked her at times if this bothers her. She always has a good attitude and says, "It makes me special."

Scars

Scars are memories that cannot be erased. They remind you of who you are. They make you stand out from the crowd. Scars remind you that there is a Creator, and He has made your amazing body to heal itself. Yes, the scars are still there, but there they remain as a beautiful reminder that cuts and wounds do heal.

Just so with your daily life, you are continuously falling, failing, and getting spiritual cuts every day, but God always heals them as long as you are willing to not pick at the scabs as they are formed. Yes, God does heal, but He always leaves little scars so that when you are having a not so wonderful day, you will always remember what God has done for you, and then you stop focusing on yourself and start focusing on God and other people.

Adelynn (Fourteen)

Yes, our family has scars, but was I going to continue picking at them instead of letting God heal them? No, I wanted my healed scars to remind me of who I am and where God brought me from. My scars are beautiful, and I need to bravely and unashamedly show them to the world. My daughter taught me a profound lesson that will forever be in my heart.

The most amazing thing was, the more I wrote my story the more God wrote through me. And the more I wrote, the more I saw my weaknesses. Many times through my writing process I would cry out to God asking him to heal me, change me and make me a better person.

If sharing my story is the key that helps just one person escape from their own prison, then the effort is all worth it! Please know that *you* were the main reason I courageously bore my scars. I know that as you read, God will meet you where you are and embrace you with His most powerful love and forgiveness, so that you will learn to *dance* upon all your pain and hopelessness and live a victorious life.

I do boldly share some painful details about my former husband, but my heart is not to be vindictive towards him in any way. We are now all walking in forgiveness. I have changed his name and sent him the raw, unedited version of my manuscript so he would be aware of everything I was writing. Miraculously, he told me and our kids, "If God showed you to write a book then who am I to stop you?" This was a huge answer to prayer. I know there are two sides to every story. I used my journal entries, past emails and memories from my children, family, and other people who walked this journey with me to make sure everything I say is as honest and accurate as possible.

There are a few stories that happened that I couldn't remember the exact time frame of when they happened but since not knowing the date didn't affect the validity and the integrity of my story, I kept them in the book. I gave actual dates of major events so you would have an idea of the timeline of when things happened. I specifically quote scriptures throughout the whole book so you will see that God's Word really does have an answer for every situation you are going through.

PART I
THE DECISION

*"You never know how strong you are
until being strong is the only **choice** you have."*

Bob Marley

CHAPTER 1
Pretense in the Parsonage

It's time to leave, I heard God whisper in my spirit.

My heart began to beat faster. *Can I really do this, God?* I prayed. *Can I really take our five children and just leave?*

Our water had been turned off for over three days. We had very little food left, and there was no money in our church account nor in our personal account to pay any of our bills. Troy's job selling mobile homes was strictly commission based, and he had not made any money in weeks. Church attendance was down to only a few people, and our power was scheduled to be turned off any day.

"Mommy, I have to go potty," Audrynn said, jumping up and down trying to hold it in. I took her to both bathrooms and realized that the toilets were stopped up with no way to flush. An overwhelming fear and hopelessness began to grip me. *Help me, God,* I cried, trying to hide the tears from my kids.

Troy had already left for work that Monday morning. I told the kids to grab all the water bottles and get in the truck so we could drive to our church and fill them up at the outside spigot. Pulling into the dirt driveway of our little church building was bitter sweet. We created so many memories there. Quality families attended our church and showered us with God's love.

Every Sunday our kids looked forward to sitting in the front row praising Jesus and listening to their daddy preach. Adelynn would dance all over the altar area without any inhibitions, and Audrynn would follow right alongside her. Dalton would passionately sing at the top of his lungs and Weston loved to help with the soundboard and the projector in the back. The delicious potlucks in the fellowship hall after church were the highlight of the week.

While I filled the bottles, my tear filled eyes scanned our church property. To think that my husband was the pastor of a church, with such a large piece of property, was very humbling. There was so much potential for growth. The kids loved to play on every part of our undeveloped twenty-five acres. They rode dune buggies, fished in the pond, collected bugs and rocks and feathers, and even put up a tent so they could have a sleep over right on church property.

As I drove back from the church, I reluctantly told the kids I really felt God showed me that we needed to leave Florida for a little while so we could take some of the stress off daddy.

Weston was twelve, Adelynn nine, Dalton seven, Audrynn four, and Azaliah ten months old. You could have heard a pin drop. I was so amazed how each of them had an unbelievable peace and understanding about it all.

"Where are we going?" Weston asked.

"Ohio," I said. I told them my dad had called me the week before and told me we could stay with them.

My dad calling was truly a defining moment in my life. During our conversation, he shared with me that as he was praying, God kept showing him he needed to help me out. Dad saw himself jumping different sized valleys with someone on his back, so he asked God who was on his back.

God said, "Your daughter is in the valley, and I want you to rescue her. I will help you to help her jump her valleys."

My dad told me he would pay for our drive home and that we could live with him and my mom for however long we needed.

This was huge, because even though my parents saw the dysfunction in our home many times, they never tried to cause any division in our marriage. Furthermore, Dad's call to me was a confirmation that God was guiding my feet every step of the way.

When we got home, the older kids excitedly ran to pack their suitcases while I went to unstop the toilets with the bottles of water.

In the meantime, Azaliah kept pulling on my shirt saying, "Mommy milk." At ten months old, she was very active and independent yet still loved to nurse quite often. It was such a beautiful experience to feed her perfect nutrition from my own body. Already in her short life, she was a living miracle and testimony of God's healing power. I felt so honored to be her mother.

This feeling wasn't always the case. When I first found out I was pregnant with her, I was completely devastated. I couldn't believe God would bring another child into our home when it was already so toxic. I am passionate about children and always wanted a house full of them. However at the time, I was deeply grieving my marriage more than ever. So the thought of adding a fifth child to take care of was overwhelming and frightening to me. In fact, an unexplained sorrow and despair began to take root in my heart. For many months I tried to break free from it.

About six months into my pregnancy, I started to bleed. I had never bled with any of my other pregnancies, so I panicked. Thankfully, Troy was home at the time and took me to see my midwife. She said the baby had a healthy heartbeat, but she still wanted us to get an ultrasound. When that chilly gel and transducer touched my belly, I immediately saw on the screen our little one, fully developed and healthy.

The most remarkable thing was that she actually had her tiny hands folded together as if she was praying for me. I couldn't believe it! I began to cry as the presence of God filled that little ultrasound room. I believe God spared the life of our little girl and reminded me in a unique way that life isn't about me, and that my children desperately needed me to be their mommy no matter how hopeless my marriage was. That day I wrote the following in my prayer journal:

March 30, 2008

Jesus, I want to thank you from the bottom of my heart for infusing me with hope and courage today. Seeing my precious baby girl gave me a new desire to fight. Please forgive me for allowing my stress and pain to rule me. I realize now that I have had a "poor me" attitude.

Thank you for showing me the Scripture in Isaiah 60:1: "Arise [from spiritual depression to a new life], shine [be radiant with the glory and brilliance of the Lord]; for your light has come, And the glory and brilliance of the Lord has risen upon you."

I am alive, and the chains of depression and sorrow have been broken off of me. I now have unexplainable confidence in knowing that with Your amazing Grace, I can rise above it all.

After I finished nursing, I went to check on the other kids. They were outside playing in our big back yard. *I can't believe we've already lived here for three years,* I thought. I remembered so vividly when we arrived as the new senior pastor's family.

Troy had been on staff at a great church for ten years prior to this and had been given many pastoral positions, but eventually he felt called to branch out and start his own ministry. He fasted for many days and felt he was ready to take on the responsibility of his own church. After accepting the senior pastor position at this church, we were so hopeful and excited to put the past behind us and "live our dream." Troy preferred to be on the front lines, doing the pastoring and wanted me to stay in the background taking care of our home and children.

The church board graciously let us live in the parsonage that belonged to the church. It was only five miles from the church building. The house was one thousand square feet with three bedrooms, two full baths, and a fourth bedroom in the former garage.

My parents had a fifth-wheel camper they would park in our back yard for three months in the winter time so they could spend time with us and help at the church. We all looked forward to Papa and Mamaw coming. Each child had the opportunity to spend the night with them. They would pack their suitcase and pretend they were taking a trip to a far-away land. In reality, they just stepped into their own back yard. Watching movies, playing games, cooking, and reading together encouraged us all on so many levels.

We lived just fifteen minutes from six thousand acres of pristine national forest and our all-time favorite place to visit, the local state park. It was home to a magnificent, spring fed lake. We swam in the pure, vibrant water on hot days, sometimes even with a herd of manatee. We took boat tours and enjoyed the sights of alligators, turtles, otters, bald eagles, and a variety of other bird species. The scenery was breathtaking. It was so thrilling for me as a homeschooling mom to be able to learn alongside my children about history and God's creation, right in the comfort of our own hometown. These fun times offered us a temporary escape from the dysfunction we felt and gave us many unbelievable memories that will be etched in our minds forever.

Married life hasn't been all *bad,* I thought to myself. The births of our five children and the true honor of being a stay at home mom are blessings I wouldn't trade for the world. Troy was a good dad. In his free time, he would play and wrestle with the kids. Their favorite play was when he would give them mustache rashes with his goatee. He didn't mind doing dishes or changing a diaper here and there. Troy was very strict with discipline and would try to have Bible studies with us as much as possible. Even though many times they were afraid of his reactions to things, the kids really loved Troy and looked forward to spending time with their daddy. Troy was exceptionally talented as a singer, songwriter, and preacher. Over the years he had the privilege to minister to many people and be surrounded by popular patriarchs and matriarchs of the faith. At times he could be the most loving, kind, and charming husband.

Maybe that is why over our fifteen years of marriage I never mentioned the abuse that was going on behind closed doors or maybe it was because the abuse came in such subtle, coercive ways and with very confusing voices. Sometimes it would be a twisting of God's Word, emotional manipulation or verbal threats that made me feel very inadequate as a wife and mother.

I did not take my marriage lightly. Never once did I think of myself as an "abused" wife, nor did I gossip to our children or to others about Troy. He was not a monster. I loved him. I read the Bible and many books on marriage and family and tried daily to apply what I was reading to my life. More than anything, I wanted to live a life that was pleasing to God and to my husband.

Writing in my journal was my outlet and lifeline. It was healing for me to be able to cry, vent, and yell just using my pen. After writing, I would usually end up having such an inner peace and much greater perspective on things.

Over the years I tried to confront Troy in private and tell him how I felt. Many times I pleaded with him to see if we could sit down with counselors or some of our close pastoral friends and really get to the root of our problems. But the few times we did finally talk with counselors, our conversations ended up only being about surface things. Troy would never mention what was really going on behind closed doors. I longed for him to be the one who told. I wanted him to fight for us.

Troy would tell us all the time, "What happens at home stays at home," and "I am the head of this house, and you will obey me." Though many times I failed, my heart wanted to respect and honor my husband at all times. Submission and obedience were extremely important to him and to me that I chose to keep quiet. Sadly and without even realizing it, the more I kept quiet, the more I became a prisoner to the hypocrisy, pride, and insecurity that daily bombarded us.

Azaliah began to get fussy which made me realize it was getting late. I went into our bedroom to lay her down and to quietly start packing. There, memories of that fateful night just a few months earlier haunted my mind.

Troy had come home from work very stressed and on edge. I should have waited to ask him, since I had already asked him earlier that week. But I needed to let the principal of the school know by the next morning if Weston was going to take the free math tutoring class. After dinner I decided to ask him again. He got angry with me. He pushed me into our bedroom and grabbed his leather belt.

"Help me, God!" I cried. But Troy repeatedly hit me with the belt.

"Please stop," I cried in anguish.

He was so strong and the more I struggled to get away, the tighter he held me. I submitted to the beating. After about three or four blows, he loosened his grip and I finally got away and ran toward the bedroom door to try to escape.

"I need to go to the bathroom," I said. He grabbed me and pushed me against the wall, choking me and holding my mouth closed. He yelled terrible, hurtful words. I looked up and saw a glimpse of his eyes, full of rage and hate, and at that moment an overwhelming fear embraced me. I finally broke free from his grasp, ran, and locked myself in the bathroom. With my heart pounding in my chest, I fell to the floor, shaking uncontrollably, and prayed. *Should I call 911? I don't want to defame his character. He is a pastor, God, but I'm so scared.*

I heard Troy yelling at all the kids, "I just spanked your mom. I am taking her down to the court house tomorrow and divorcing her, and if you all don't shape up, I am spanking you next."

Weston, who was only twelve, began crying and said, "No, please don't!" A supernatural strength rose up inside of me. I ran out of that bathroom and yelled at Troy to leave the kids alone. Weston continued crying and said he was having chest pains and couldn't breathe. After hearing that, Troy left. I comforted Weston for a while and then went to check on the others. My heart broke when I found Adelynn and Dalton in a closet, hugging each other. Thankfully, Audrynn and Azaliah slept through the whole thing. While he was gone I called my parents asking them to pray.

Troy came back home that night acting as if nothing had happened. He felt bad that he upset the kids, but he told me that my dad should have done what he did to me years ago. To say the least, I was completely devastated.

If only these walls could talk, I cried out to God. *I am so tired of living a secret life! God,* I yelled inside, *these chains of hypocrisy and fear are choking the very life out of me and rendering me completely powerless. I want to be free! Jesus, please give me the courage to overcome, the grace to let go, and the strength to tell the truth.*

The next day Troy did not take me down to the courthouse and that night we had a Valentine's Day dinner at our church. I didn't want to go, but Troy said, "You are going!"

As I was waiting for a table, that old familiar feeling of despair and loneliness started consuming me all over again. I wanted to run away! In fact, if I didn't have Azaliah on my lap, I know I would really have done it. Every time I thought about the incident of the night before and the devastation of our failing marriage, I would literally lose my breath and begin to cry.

Watching Troy eating and hearing him talking and laughing with his church family made me sick to my stomach. I continually had to excuse myself to go the bathroom to try to gain control so no one would see in my eyes the deep rooted sorrow and grief that was tormenting my soul. I was the pastor's wife; I had to be strong.

When I got home and put the kids to bed, I went to take a walk around our neighborhood. I was desperately crying out to God to give me a word, a way of escape, anything to take away the utter despair I was feeling. Years of living in such turmoil and the many threats of divorce had taken their toll on me. I needed immediate help. Sadly as a pastor's wife, I felt I had nowhere to turn but to God.

Looking up at the night sky made me feel so close to God. The contrast of the clear, black sky and the white stars proclaimed so loudly God's incredible handiwork, which reassured me that He heard me and was with me.

A few days later I was reading my Bible and happened to open it to Ezekiel 12:1–6:

> "Then the word of the Lord came to me, saying, "Son of man, you live in the midst of the rebellious house, who have eyes to see but do not see, ears to hear but do not hear; for they are a rebellious house. Therefore, son of man, prepare for yourself baggage for exile and go into exile by day in their sight; even go into exile from your place to another place in their sight. Perhaps they will understand though they are a rebellious house." (NASB)

I couldn't believe it. Without a shadow of doubt, God spoke to me so clearly. I had never noticed that passage before. God wanted me to leave temporarily in the hope that my husband would see the hurt he was causing his family. I cried out asking God to give me confirmation because I knew He always confirms His Word.

Just a week or so later, a strong married couple from our church came up to me. The husband said, "Look me in the eyes. I want to know, is your husband treating you right?"

I hesitated but told him, "Yes." He saw my hesitation and explained to me what it said in 1 Peter 3:7:

> "In the same way, you husbands, live with your wives in an understanding way [with great gentleness and tact, and with an intelligent regard for the marriage relationship], as with someone physically weaker, since she is a woman. Show her honor and respect as a fellow heir of the grace of life, so that your prayers will not be hindered or ineffective."

He continued telling me that if Troy wasn't treating me right, then his prayers wouldn't be answered, and this church wouldn't grow. I was dumfounded when the husband told me this because never once had our family displayed any strife or dysfunction publicly.

As I pondered these confirmations, I realized that undoubtedly God was serving as my husband and my defender! It was then that I knew that just like it says in Matthew18, beyond any shadow of a doubt it was time for me to be brave and tell a few trustworthy people who knew Troy the real story.

> "If your brother sins, go and show him his fault in private; if he listens and pays attention to you, you have won back your brother. But if he does not listen, take along with you one or two others, so that every word may be confirmed by the testimony of two or three witnesses. If he pays no attention to them [refusing to listen and obey], tell it to the church; and if he refuses to listen even to the church, let him be to you as a Gentile (unbeliever) and a tax collector" Matthew 18:15–17

Many times I would grieve for my husband and have such a compassion for him. The insurmountable pressure of trying to be the perfect pastor, having a perfect family, and competing with our culture was extremely stressful on him. I think he thought that if he shared what was really happening behind closed doors he would receive no grace, and it would be the death of his life-long dream. He was afraid to fail. So in his eyes, denial was the only option.

I finally got up the nerve and bravely called one of our close pastor friends and briefly shared with them the highlights of the abuse that happened that night and the dysfunction that had wreaked havoc in our marriage over the years. I was intensely nervous. I did not want to exaggerate anything, blame him for everything, or defame my husband's name unnecessarily. My main goal in telling was to hopefully bring complete restoration to my family!

Miraculously, the more I shared my heart, the more God gave me the courage to overcome. I literally felt the thick chains of pride and fear that had gripped me for so many years start to dissolve, and a huge burden was lifted off of me.

It was immensely encouraging to see with my own eyes the Scripture in Revelation 12:11 really come alive in my personal situation:

"And they overcame him because of the blood of the Lamb and because of the word of their testimony, and they did not love their life even when faced with death" (NASB).

Thankfully, our pastor friend and his wife counseled us. Unfortunately, circumstances just got worse. Troy's anger and control reached a new level. He took my church key and said I could no longer go to the church without him. I had no internet access, and I wasn't allowed to go anywhere without his permission. He told me I was no longer allowed to write in my journals and that he was going to throw them all in a fire and burn them.

Even though through human eyes things looked hopeless, I felt such a relief and a beautiful freedom! I no longer had to pretend that we were a perfect family anymore.

Malachi 2:14–16 was another profound confirmation that I was hearing from God and doing the right thing:

> "But you say, 'Why does He reject it?' Because the Lord has been a witness between you and the wife of your youth, against whom you have dealt treacherously. Yet she is your marriage companion and the wife of your covenant made by your vows.

> "But not one has done so who has a remnant of the Spirit. And what did that one do while seeking a godly offspring? Take heed then to your spirit, and let no one deal treacherously against the wife of your youth."

> "For I hate divorce," says the Lord, the God of Israel, "and him who covers his garment with wrong and violence," says the Lord of hosts. "Therefore keep watch on your spirit, so that you do not deal treacherously with your wife."

The buzzer on the timer went off; telling me that the banana bread I was baking for our trip was ready to come out of the oven. I glanced at the clock on the stove and couldn't believe what time it was already—10:00 a.m. I quickly finished packing all of our necessities and anxiously told the kids to help me load the truck. I didn't want Troy to come home in the midst of us leaving. Weston was such a good helper. He assisted me by loading all the little bikes, our high chair, stroller, a few favorite toys, and suitcases into the back of our truck.

Thankfully, we had a Ford F-150 King Cab that sat three in the front and three in the back. We all quickly buckled in. Weston and the baby in a rear facing car seat were up front, and Adelynn, Dalton, and Audrynn were in the back.

It was June 9, 2009. With a big sigh of relief, I prayed, *I am taking my children to Ohio. God, I desperately plead with You to minister to Troy and me both while we are away from each other. Give us wisdom, direction, and healing, so that our marriage will be restored and our family will be back together again soon.*

As I drove off, I briefly glanced in the rearview mirror and saw my children's little eyes looking up with such trust and innocence. Instantly I realized the magnitude of this journey in so many lives. I said another prayer under my breath and called my dad to tell him we were on our way.

CHAPTER 2
The Journey Home

It was such a beautiful, sunny day to drive. The older kids were listening to adventure mysteries on CDs about creation versus evolution, while Audrynn and Azaliah were sleeping off and on, or playing with their toys and eating snacks. They were all being extremely well behaved.

Throughout the drive, I tried to engage myself in listening to the many CDs just to keep my mind off things. But sadness and grief were so present that all I could think about was my pain and memories of my past.

What do you want to be when you grow up? "A wife and mother," would always be my response. From the time I could remember, I always had such an insatiable desire to learn everything I could about raising my own family. I adored children and babysat all the time.

Throughout the years I read many books on marriage and family. I was also truly blessed to have parents who raised me to know God and modeled not a perfect, but a healthy marriage in front of me. My family tree was very fascinating to me. I desperately wanted to continue the legacy that my great grandparents,

grandparents, and parents left for me, to be married for life and to raise my children to know God.

Some of my fondest memories of childhood were the times when my Dad, mom, brother, sister, and I, faithfully visited the tiny grave yard every year in southern Ohio, to put flowers on the tombstones. All of my father's side of the family is buried there. I would run from grave to grave fervently reading the names on each tombstone and asking my parents many questions about each one of these family member's lives.

I even had a desire to marry a pastor one day. When I was sixteen years old, my brother came into my room and asked me what I was reading. *"Help! I'm a Pastor's Wife,"* I replied.[1] He started laughing and teased me about it, as brothers do, for many months after that.

In high school playing sports was definitely a passion and even to this day if you put a ball in my hand, I will play for hours. I played softball, basketball, and volleyball. During my senior year in high school, I was offered the chance to receive a volleyball scholarship. After much prayer, I turned it down and chose to go to Bible College.

I majored in the ministry of helps. I wanted to learn more about how to serve, not only my church family, but also my future husband and children. I really believed that my calling was to be an armor bearer for my husband, whoever he might be. I wanted to serve my future family and one day make my own home a haven and a refuge for all who might walk through our doors. All the classes I took were geared towards this main goal.

During the years I was at Bible College, my parents wanted me to still live with them, which I thought was a great honor. I was eighteen years old, and although it was difficult, I chose not to date anyone. I wanted to completely focus on my studies and develop a deeper relationship with Jesus Christ.

During my third year of Bible College, I met Troy who worked in the cubicle right beside mine. I took a job to defray

---

1 Michael O'Donnell, *Help! I'm a Pastor's Wife* (Nashville: Thomas Nelson, 1992).

the cost of my school and living. Troy and I became immediate friends. He told me he wanted to be a eunuch because he had just ended a serious five-year relationship. I teasingly told him I wanted to be a nun. We talked all the time about different things, and much to my delight, I found out that he came all the way from Florida to attend the same Bible College as me. I couldn't believe it.

Troy and I continued to communicate and finally he decided to ask my dad if he could date me. My dad said, "Erica is her own person, and she will do whatever God shows her. But you have my blessing to date her." My parents adored Troy. God gave them a supernatural love for him as if he were their own son. Troy asked me to dinner that next weekend and of course I said yes. In the meantime, our church's praise and worship pastor and director of the music school sold Troy his little green convertible Fiat for really cheap. On a beautiful Saturday evening, Troy picked me up in his little sports car with the top down. We drove to a quaint little restaurant / ice cream shop. Thus began our relationship. After dating for one year and finally getting both of our parents' and our pastor's permission, Troy asked me to marry him.

My wedding day had finally arrived, the day I had been waiting for my whole life. I was twenty-two years old and was honored to be able to vow to my man that I would love him until death do us part. I was ecstatic to have found the perfect white dress. It had puffy sleeves, an empire waist, and intricate beading woven throughout the top of it. After putting it on, I looked in the mirror and immediately felt like the most beautiful, pure princess in the whole world. In the dressing room I had my precious godly mother, my six amazing bridesmaids and one junior bridesmaid surrounding me. I felt such love and support that I didn't ever want to leave that room.

In my wedding dress I was excited to present myself to my dad for the first time. I was waiting for him in the big sanctuary. The minute he opened the door from the usher's room and saw me, tears began to flood his eyes. He looked at me with such a love and admiration that I began to laugh. It was not just an ordinary laugh, but a laugh that came from the inner-most parts of my being because in that moment, a beautiful new bonding took place between my father and me. I was so honored and privileged that Dad would be the one walking me down the aisle.

Troy had written a song before we met about the bride of Christ and wanted to sing it to me. Walking down the aisle, with my dad on one arm and my Father God on the other, while Troy sang was an experience I will treasure in my heart forever. In that moment, I felt the pure, unadulterated presence of God surround me and the tangible love of God embrace me.

When I met Troy at the altar, my pastor whispered in my ear that I was the most beautiful bride he had ever seen. His words will stay with me forever because I knew he saw Jesus in me and my prayer to give myself to my husband as a pure and holy bride had been answered.

"Mommy, Mommy, look at that huge rocket!" Dalton yelled loudly. I couldn't believe we had already made it to the halfway mark, Huntsville, Alabama. We stopped at a Welcome Center so we could stretch our legs and go to the bathroom. I am so glad we did because the huge rocket Dalton had seen off the inter-state was a monument there. After we had gone to the bathroom and I changed Azaliah's diaper, the kids ran over to look at it.

Weston's favorite subject was history. He read all about the rocket on the plaques. The 224 foot Saturn 1B rockets had been used for missions in the Apollo space program. The little ones were mesmerized by how massive it was. They kept running all around it pretending they were astronauts. The rocket was per-fect for temporarily keeping our minds distracted from what was really happening in our lives.

But as we were getting back in the truck to leave, I started doubting my decision, thinking, *Maybe this wasn't the right thing to do? I probably should turn back around?* I started to call Troy. I really wanted his permission. I picked up my phone several times to dial but hung up right before I did. Eventually, I got up the nerve and called him.

"Troy, I want you to know that I have taken the kids and left. I wrote a letter to you and left it on your. . ."

Before I could finish my sentence, he started yelling, "Turn that truck around immediately and come back home! You have no right to just leave without me knowing. If you don't come back, you will be sorry!"

In that brief moment I felt guilt, fear, and control trying to grip me all over again. But instead of succumbing to it, a surprising courage arose within my soul, and with God's help, I continued driving to Ohio. Many times my phone rang, but I just turned up my praise music and ignored the ringing, praying continuously for God's strength and protection to make it to our destination.

I was so thankful my dad paid for us to stay in a hotel, because after about eight hours, I was really tired of driving. The kids were starting to get restless, and Azaliah had been whining off and on since we left the rest area. I decided to stop in Nashville, Tennessee and surprised the kids by stopping at a Cracker Barrel to eat. If I could have bottled the huge, radiant smiles on their faces, I would have. Each one was thrilled to eat at such a fun restaurant.

After we finished eating, I drove to the nearest reasonably priced hotel. The kids started screaming because they were all overjoyed to be staying in a hotel. I could count on one hand the number of times we were privileged to stay in one.

The kids absolutely loved the water and were all avid swimmers. Even the baby would wear her armies and swim like a fish. When we found out the hotel had a pool, they begged me to take them swimming. It was past 8:00 p.m. and I was utterly exhausted. So I promised that we would get a late check out and go swimming in the morning.

Weston and Adelynn got some snacks ready to eat while I helped everyone else take hot baths and get their cozy pajamas on. We didn't have cable television at home, so the kids were thrilled to watch a few children's shows before they went to bed. I prayed before I fell asleep that it wouldn't rain and that no one would steal our stuff, since it was all packed in the back of our open bed truck with no tarp over it.

Amazingly, we all had a great night sleep, it didn't rain one drop, and no one stole anything. We hurriedly packed our suitcases and ate a continental breakfast. I was so tempted to just get on the road and not go swimming, but I forced myself to keep my word. It was comical to watch people's reactions when they saw me swimming with my many children. The famous comments were always, "Are these all yours?" and "You sure have your hands full!" I am so glad we went swimming because it provided another distraction to ease our tension. It helped bond us more together, and thankfully, it made the kids more relaxed and tired for our long drive ahead.

After about six hours of driving, it was very motivating to see in the distance the huge suspension bridge that crosses over the Ohio River into Cincinnati! When I drove from Kentucky into Ohio it felt like I was driving into freedom. Excitement and hope overwhelmed me. Knowing I was finally in my home state brought me to tears. I couldn't believe we only had two hours left of driving.

Even though the many stops to "go potty" ended up making the final leg of our trip much longer than I expected, overall I was so proud of the kids. Without TV to entertain them, they were so creative entertaining themselves with coloring, reading, listening to stories on CD, and best of all, not fighting. Their behavior blessed me so much, and I made sure they knew it.

After about eighteen hours of driving over two days, I was elated to finally reach my parent's drive way. I got out of the truck and fell on their plush green grass, praising God that we made it without any complications or rain. My mom and dad ran out and greeted us. While hugging my mom, I started crying and wouldn't let go of her. In that moment I felt so relieved, so safe, and so loved.

It was getting very late, and my dad suggested we put a tarp over our truck and wait until the next morning to unload everything. My parents had a little three bedroom duplex, and one of the bedrooms was an office, so trying to figure out sleeping arrangements was interesting. The office had a murphy bed that pulled out from the wall that Weston slept on and the rest of us slept in the guest bedroom. Adelynn and Dalton slept on the floor in sleeping bags while Audrynn, Azaliah, and I slept on the queen size bed. It worked out perfectly because I wanted my kids to be as close to me as possible.

As I laid my head down on my pillow to go to sleep, I found it extremely hard to relax. I had many anxious emotions and thoughts running rampant in my mind. I kept rehearsing over and over the why's and how's of my failing marriage. Listening to the rhythm of all my little ones breathing while they were asleep comforted me, gave me peace, and helped to ease my tension.

Really, from the beginning our marriage was rocky, I thought to myself while staring up at the bedroom ceiling. I was excited and hopeful to start living my dream as a helpmeet to my new husband. I loved to decorate. Our little apartment was very cute. The kitchen had an apple theme, and our bedroom was highly inviting. We found a six piece, massive Paul Bunyan bedroom suit at a garage sale that we fell in love with. The bed had four huge posts that made me feel like royalty every time I walked in the room and our living room had brand new plaid couches that tied all of our favorite colors together. During this time I was able to work as a bank teller while Troy pursued his calling as an assistant youth pastor at the church we got married in.

However, since I was married right out of my home at a young age, I had never really mastered the art of cooking and cleaning. Troy was seven years older than me and had lived on his own for over ten years. He was a great cook and came from a family of wonderful cooks. He also really loved coming home to a clean house with dinner on the table. To say the least, I failed many times. A few weeks after we were married, Troy came home, and the house wasn't cleaned to his liking, and the potato soup was

21

burnt. He got uncommonly mad and kicked our kitchen table bench so hard it put a hole in the wall. This was very frightening and alarming to me because the whole time we dated, I only saw Troy get angry one time. He got into an ugly fist fight with his roommate over money. I also had very rarely seen my parents fight and I definitely had never seen my dad get that angry with my mom.

In just a few short months, strife was a common occurrence in our marriage. Troy would yell and I would defend myself and cry. On many occasions I would run to my closet in desperation, burying my face in the carpet begging God to help me. I began to feel very inadequate and insecure as his wife. I blamed myself and was desperate to find out how I could become better so my husband would love me more and not get so angry. After about a year of marriage was when I started having a strong desire for children. I thought having a baby might help Troy love me more and help me to have more confidence in who I was as his wife.

CHAPTER 3
Stopped Dead in My Tracks

Waking up the next morning with the sun peering through the blinds, shining on my children's faces while they slept, made me so grateful to be under my dad's roof again. I felt so protected and loved, but for some reason, fear and guilt were still trying to control me. *What was I thinking, taking our children hundreds of miles away without Troy's permission?* I thought. I knew deep down that he was still very angry, so I waited for him to call me.

A week or so went by and I finally got a phone call from him. He was indeed very angry. He told me that taking the kids and leaving forced him to resign as the pastor of his church. Then he commanded me to come back home right away. His words of blame pierced me like a knife. I tried to argue with him and defend myself but to no avail. Even though there were only a couple members left in the church and there was no money left in the church account, I still felt so terrible that he blamed me for his resignation. I began doubting my decision to leave. I even started to plot out many different scenarios of how the kids and I could go back to Florida. My dad was such a wealth of wisdom, so I shared with him the things Troy had said. Then I told him I thought that maybe I should take the kids back to Florida.

My dad said, "Until he is truly sorry for how he has treated his family and proves it to you, you have nothing to gain and everything to lose if you go back to him."

After much pondering on what my dad said, I still felt that I should pack up the kids and head back to Florida. I left Ohio praying that God would stop me in my tracks if we were not supposed to go. Unbeknownst to me at the time, my parents were praying the same thing.

Before heading back to Florida, we went to go see my brother, David. I missed him and his family and very rarely got to see them. We had a great time together. Like my dad, David cautioned me and told me I shouldn't go back to Troy. No matter what my decision was to be, he was still very thoughtful and made sure my truck was road worthy. He listened to the engine and checked the oil, brakes, and tires and said we were good to go.

I was about sixty miles down the road when all of a sudden the truck started shaking and we heard a loud noise. I immediately pulled to the side of the road; got out of the truck and realized a tire blew out. Crying, I called my brother and he told me he was on his way. While waiting for David, I felt Jesus' love and peace fill our truck in the most tangible way. Astonishingly, the nagging guilt and fear that had been tormenting me since we left Florida instantaneously left me.

With a new found hope and clarity, I looked back at my children and said, "Do you realize what just happened? Jesus loves us so much that He stopped our truck from driving back to Florida because He knew that daddy was not ready to have us back yet."

David tried to put on the spare tire, but it was blown out too. We had to try and find a tire store. We were out in the middle of nowhere. It was an ordeal and quite comical trying to fit five kids in his little hatch back so we could search for a tire place. We were eventually able to find one about thirty miles down the road. David bought the tire, brought it back and put it on the truck. I was so thankful that my brother was able to rescue us. Since I was terrible with directions, he told me adamantly to head east and not south and made sure I knew the way back to mom and dad's house.

As I was driving back to my parent's house, I praised God for His loving protection and His sovereignty. I praised Him for the beautiful, teachable moment that I had with the kids. I praised Him for the unexplainable peace of knowing, for the time being, living with my parents was right where God wanted me.

Over the next few months I talked to Troy many times on the telephone and tried to work things out. However, our communication was still full of anger and blame. Many times I would hang up feeling extremely discouraged and hopeless. Troy refused to come to Ohio, even for a visit. We had the perfect set up. My parents did not mind if Troy stayed with us until we healed and got back on our feet. They even offered to watch the kids while we went to counseling. Troy's excuse for not coming was, "Ohio is *your* stomping grounds."

At one point, Troy called to tell me that he was moving to Texas on the advice of one of his longtime friends who lived there. His friend told Troy the job opportunities were much better and the church he was on staff at had world renowned marriage counseling. After hearing this, I was extremely relieved and hopeful. Even though Troy was not offered a job, this event was a huge answer to prayer! I ran to tell my parents. We were all thrilled that Troy now had a godly support system, accountability and most importantly we had great marriage counselors to go to.

Troy and I had conference calls a few times with our friend who offered to pay my way to Texas so Troy and I could meet with a marriage counselor.

I decided to take Azaliah with me since she was still nursing and had severe separation anxiety. My parents wouldn't have been able to handle five kids, let alone one screaming the whole time. Thankfully, there was no charge, as long as she sat on my lap for the flight.

My dad drove us to the airport, actually parked and walked us in. He made sure I was all checked in. When they called my flight number, he gave me a big hug. With tears in his eyes, he kissed my cheek. I was speechless. My dad loved me so much, but rarely did he show physical affection. That kiss stayed with me for a long time and gave me a new courage I so desperately needed.

In Texas, Troy and I went to marriage counseling together. God gave me the grace to share everything, even the abuse. Troy shared some too. We both began crying and we told each other we were sorry. The counselor gave us some excellent advice and reading materials. One of those was the book called, "Angry Men and the Women who love them[2]." He recommended that Troy continue counseling with him in Texas and that I go to counseling in Ohio. I left Texas somewhat hopeful about the possibility of reconciliation. At the same time I was troubled. Troy never mentioned any of the abuse he did in the past. He was sorry that he lost his church and family, but he still felt justified for how he treated me and he still felt that I deserved every bit of it.

Even though Troy still did not have a job, he told me while I was in Texas with him that he wanted me and the kids to move to Texas as soon as possible. Together we looked at different housing in the suburbs, for a possible place to live. Since we could no longer live in the parsonage, he said that he was going to go through all of our stuff when he got back to Florida and get rid of everything except for our much needed things. He said he was then going to put our belongings in a storage shed in Texas.

A few weeks later I talked to Troy. He told me that he stopped going to counseling because the counselor did not want to meet with him anymore. I emailed his counselor and he told me that what Troy said was not true. He said Troy never showed up for any of his scheduled sessions. After finding that out, I was completely devastated.

Troy then turned off my cell phone, telling me that I didn't answer it quick enough. He eventually cut off all communication with everybody. Many weeks went by with no calls or emails.

2 Paul Hegstorm, Angry Men and the Women Who Love Them: Breaking the Cycle of Physical and Emotional Abuse [Kansas City, Beacon Hill Press: Revised edition 2004]

I talked to friends and family to see if anyone had heard from him, but no one had.

Seeing how much the kids missed their daddy was killing me. They had not seen him since we left, which had been nearly four months by now. Adelynn missed her daddy so much that she refused to take off her pink shirt that Troy had gotten her that said, "Daddy's little girl" on it. The times I did make her take it off so I could wash it, she would immediately put it right back on. This broke my heart. She was trying to be as close to her daddy as she possibly could.

One time after a long night of trying to get Azaliah to sleep, I went to go to the bathroom and wash my hands. I happened to glance up at myself in the mirror and was horrified by the hideous dark circles under my eyes. In that moment, reality hit me like a baseball bat. *I am a single mom. How will I ever be able to provide for* five *children?* I thought. I wrote the following in my prayer journal:

October 31, 2009

I am so distraught. We feel abandoned in every way. Troy turned off my cell phone, doesn't call and doesn't send any letters or money. I feel hopeless. I am mad at you, God. I thought you were going to save my marriage. The kids are so sad and need their daddy. I don't know who I am or what I am doing anymore. I am angry and hurt. Sometimes I even take it out on the kids, which I feel terrible about. God, please forgive me for yelling and reacting in anger and for trying to do so many things in my own strength. I feel like such a burden to my parents. Please help me!

Many nights I would cry myself to sleep and then would barely be able to get out of bed the next morning. It took every fiber of my being to function as a mommy. The dynamics of trying to handle not only my hurting heart, but five other little hurting hearts in the midst of being extremely angry was exhausting. Not only was I emotionally and spiritually hurting, I was also physically in pain. For some reason, I would wake up all the time with severe stiff necks. I couldn't understand why. I was normally very healthy and took good care of my body. At first I tried natural remedies to take the pain away. I tried changing my pillow, ice packs, and hot showers, because I hated taking any type of medicine and tried to avoid it at all costs.

However as the weeks passed, the pain was so severe and debilitating that I would force myself to take ibuprofen. Even though we had no health insurance, I knew I had to get some help. My mom told her chiropractor about my situation. He was her close friend's son. He offered to X-ray my neck for free. I never dreamed he would say, "You have severe whiplash." He asked me if I had been in an accident in the past six months. I hesitated, but said I didn't think so.

Immediately thoughts of the night Troy tried to hold me down became so vivid. I remembered jerking my neck very hard trying to get away. I eventually told the chiropractor a few of the details of that night and thankfully he offered to do a couple of adjustments on me for free. He highly recommended that I get on a treatment plan so the injury did not get any worse. He felt I would suffer for many years without it.

To say the least, sorrow and despair were very present in our home. However, the restoration of my marriage was still continually at the forefront of my thoughts and prayers. I kept my wedding ring on at all times. I was not giving up. But even though I longed to be a whole family again, I had to face the harsh reality of the moment: I was single and parenting alone. It was time to take action and snap out of the hopelessness and fear of what that new label *single* really meant.

Therefore I was forced to make some major decisions. This was a lot harder than I thought it would be. In fact, it was quite nerve racking. First and foremost, I wanted to get our taxes done. Many years they did not get done, which was a constant torment to me. I thought the IRS was going to come and take us to jail. The Taxes were already many months past due, but this time I got the courage up to find an accountant to help me. I was so thankful that I had grabbed the W2, our vital records and some of the bills we owed when I was in Florida.

I decided to go to my parents' accountant. When he finished our taxes and told me we would be getting $4,000 back, I was in utter disbelief. I thought for sure we would owe money and have to pay a huge penalty. However, he told me that when we receive money back, there never is a penalty. I was so relieved and excited that I started thanking God for his amazing provision in our lives. I offered to give my dad some of the money to help with expenses. The water bill alone had to have doubled in size. Graciously, he told me to use it for our needs. I never could keep secrets from Troy, so the next time I finally got to talk to him I told him how I was able to receive money back from our taxes. He told me to send him some of the money so I sent him $1,000. I wanted to help him as much as I could so he could get the job and help he needed for us to become a family again.

My next major decision was to try to find a way to make an income. I had no degree and very little experience, but I refused to be a burden to my parents. At the same time, I still believed it was very important to continue to teach my children at home, like we did in Florida. Homeschooling isn't for everyone. But even before I got married, I watched many families homeschool and thought it would be so cool to be able to one day homeschool my own children. Thankfully after much prayer, Troy said yes. I was so excited and grateful to have the honor of schooling my children at home. We took Weston out of school when he was entering the third grade and thus began our homeschooling journey.

Weston was now in seventh grade, Adelynn fourth grade, and Dalton first grade. Audrynn at age four and Azaliah at fourteen months old were not in school yet. I was at a crossroads wondering what would be the most beneficial to all of us, including my parents. Should I work full time and put my kids in school, or continue teaching them at home? It was a crucial decision because I believed the most effective way to bring healing and restoration would be by keeping the kids in the same environment they were used to. Doing so would give them great continuity and a much faster healing. We would bond more as a family and learn to work together as a team instead of being segregated eight to ten hours every day. I wanted my children to know that despite what was happening, they were not a liability but a huge blessing to me. Each one daily gave me courage and motivation to keep fighting.

If I put the older ones in school and worked full time, then I would have to find full time child care for Audrynn and Azaliah. My mom offered to watch them sometimes, but everyday all day long would be too much for her. After researching the different childcare centers, I couldn't believe how expensive they were. It would take most of my paycheck just to pay the tuition. So between not being able to afford childcare and thinking about the trauma of throwing my kids in school in the midst of them trying to heal, was when I realized for the time being, keeping them all at home would be much more beneficial emotionally, physically spiritually and financially, for all of us.

However, the temptation to let someone else teach my kids was powerful! The demands of raising five children from a teenager down to toddler in the midst of us all trying to grieve and heal was so emotionally and physically draining, that many times I would literally fall apart just trying to survive.

One time Audrynn looked at me and asked, "Mommy, why do you have angry eyebrows?" Her question hit me in the gut like a ton of bricks. It opened my eyes to the reality that at times I really was taking my hurt and unforgiveness out on them. Like the counselor told me in Texas, I had to find counseling or some type of a godly support group. My reactions to my parents and my children were not normal. I was very emotional and overly defensive. I had deep rooted hurt and anger towards Troy that kept manifesting itself and definitely needed to be dealt with.

I ended up calling Focus on the Family's counseling hotline and cried out for help. They talked to me and prayed with me for over an hour and gave me some excellent advice, resources and books to help with my healing process. After hanging up with them, I felt extremely encouraged and valued. I felt God's love flowing through our conversation. It was a huge surprise when I received a few of the books they recommended in the mail for free!

The most amazing thing was that the same day I talked to Focus on the Family, my dad was watching a Christian television program. They had a guest speaker on that was talking about a six month long, Christian based, gender specific class he started for people who had been in dysfunctional and abusive relationships. When my dad said, "Hurry up and come watch this guy," I was speechless because I realized it was the same person that authored the book our counselor in Texas recommended that Troy and I read.

I immediately called the number on the screen. They were very helpful and explained all about their ministry. They then told me some names of instructors within a thirty mile radius of where I lived. The nearest instructor was just ten minutes down the road. The best part was that the instructor, Elaine, was one of my mom's lifelong friends. She had known me from the time I was a little girl. My dad graciously paid my way, so I signed up for the fall class that was starting just a few weeks later. My mom called Elaine and excitedly told her that I was going to be taking her class and shared with her the beauty of everything that fell into place.

That day I stood in utter amazement at how God was working on our behalf in such unexplainable ways. His provision and timing was impeccable and miraculous to say the least. God really does cause all things to work together for the good to those who love Him and are called according to His purpose (Rom. 8:28).

Elaine sent me all the information about the "Life Skills" class and a video depicting the life story of the class leader. That video itself brought me so much hope that I could not wait to start the class. In fact, I was so excited about it, I emailed Troy, hoping he might respond. I asked him if he wouldn't mind taking the same class in Texas. I looked it up and they actually had a men's class in the same area where he was living. Sadly, Troy ended up disregarding my message.

CHAPTER 4
Giving Up the Possibility of a Better Past

I couldn't believe it was already winter time. We had been with my parents for over six months. It was so much fun for my kids to see snow for the first time and boy, did we get a ton of snow. We had a blast throwing snow balls, building snowmen and going sledding. Watching Azaliah fearlessly climb up the hill on her little chubby legs and then slide down with her brothers and sisters was a sight I will never forget. The kids talked my mom into getting all the Christmas stuff out so we could decorate the house. It was such a joy to see my kids laugh and play, enjoying life.

I finally got a job working nights at McDonalds making minimum wage. When I went to work I would put the kids to bed before I left, then come home and sleep for a few hours, and then homeschool my three older ones. I would have the younger two watch some learning videos or color. My mom was there quite often if I needed any help.

My mom and dad were an amazing source of strength to me. They prayed for me and encouraged me relentlessly. My mom babysat at times and gave so much of her time and energy to us all. She wanted me to be a success and she was determined to do everything she could to help me accomplish my goals. Many times the messy house or the chaos of five kids running around would really frustrate her, but she handled it well. She was a great example of God's grace and power working in her life on a daily basis.

My dad was a constant, steady strength. He was the healthy father figure my kids desperately needed. His wisdom and fierce love for me, my kids and his wife gave us a tangible representation of who God really is. At times Dad would do special things with each one of the kids. He would let them watch Ohio State football with him or take them on little adventures or buy them special treats and gifts.

We all were elated when Troy started calling the kids more often. He sent the kids each a special hand-written letter and a homemade stuffed hand that said, "Hold daddy's hand," which I considered very thoughtful and creative. Troy told the kids that he was flying in for Christmas and they were beyond excited. He gave us the specific dates and the kids marked them on their calendar and began counting down the days.

Surprisingly, I also had a little twinge of excitement at the thought of seeing him again in the hope that he might be different. We had a gift for him wrapped under the tree, a brand new pair of Saucony hiking shoes. All the kids had made him special homemade cards.

At the last minute, Troy canceled and never came. The kids were devastated. I tried my best to make that Christmas memorable and fun. I even bought the kids a real bunny rabbit that they had been begging for years. But there was still such sadness and disappointment in their eyes. Thankfully, a few of Troy's brothers, sisters and his dad sent a box full of gifts that brought a temporary excitement to the kids.

Christmas came and went and reality was really starting to set in. I couldn't believe it was now the year 2010. It had been a few months since I took the nighttime position at McDonalds and my parents were utterly exhausted. Azaliah would wake up throughout the night while I was working and my mom would have to be up with her. We all were sleep deprived and on edge. My dad would spend hours in the basement in his "man cave" trying to escape the chaos and my mom was beginning to have a few anxiety attacks.

The older kids were for the most part well behaved. Little Azaliah was the one who kept us on our toes and made things a little more chaotic. She was my little monkey. She challenged us quite often. She had a tremendous amount of energy and was very athletic. Starting at only ten months old, she continually climbed out of her crib. She probably fell down the basement stairs at least three or four times, no matter what we did to try to stop her. She had a will of iron and wanted to constantly learn and do new things. Regretfully in the midst of my pain, I probably spoiled her. She was my security blanket. I would nurse her at night, which caused her to have a hard time sleeping on her own. I didn't discipline her as much as we did the others at her age.

In disciplining the kids is where I missed Troy. He expected the kids to obey the first time. He would tell the kids, "Slow obedience is no obedience." Azaliah unfortunately missed out on that training. Even though the stage she was in was hard, my parents and I still loved and adored Azaliah. Her determination and passion for life was an inspiration to us all.

I was so relieved when I found out that it was time for my parents to take their normal and much needed yearly, three-month vacation to Florida for the winter. I was a little apprehensive about it and wondered many times how I would ever juggle everything on my own. But overall I was thrilled for them to get away and be refreshed and revived.

When my parents left, I didn't have anyone to watch the kids when I went to work and to my life skills class, so I was forced to rely on Weston and Adelynn for babysitting. They were thirteen and ten. Weston was not too fond of the idea but was there in case of an emergency. Adelynn had a natural gift with children. Her nurturing personality and love for her siblings and Weston's expertise on things made them a great team to babysit the younger kids while I was gone. I would put the three little ones to bed before I went to work so Weston and Adelynn would not have to watch them, just keep an ear out for them.

Despite their best efforts, many times Adelynn called me at work saying the baby woke up, and she couldn't get her back to sleep, or the baby woke up the other ones and they were not cooperating very well. It was heart wrenching for me to have to leave my five children all alone, especially at night. This time lasted about a month until I finally had no other option than to tell my manager I could no longer work at McDonalds. This was so hard because I was not a quitter, especially since I had nothing else to fall back on. But my children and their safety were my first priority.

I called my mom and dad in Florida and told them I had to quit working. They were very understanding and told me that it would probably take time to find a way to make an income, especially in my situation. Having my parents gone was extremely difficult, but at the same time was so healthy for me. It made me have to rely on God more than ever.

I had to come to the conclusion that the McDonalds job was probably not from God. I had acted in fear, panicked, and tried to get any job that came my way instead of trusting Him to guide my footsteps. It was such a relief not to have to leave my kids home alone anymore.

"Trust in and rely confidently on the Lord with all your heart And do not rely on your own insight or understanding. In all your ways know and acknowledge and recognize Him, And He will make your paths straight and smooth [removing obstacles that block your way.]" Prov. 3:5-6

While my parents were in Florida my dad had a minor heart attack. This was very scary to me. Thankfully it was minor with no heart damage, but I sure did blame myself. I knew the stress of taking care of six extra people was taking a toll on him. My parents told us all the time that we were a blessing and not a burden and they rarely complained about anything. Their hearts wanted to help us out in whatever way they could, but sadly their emotions and their bodies were telling them something different.

Food was our biggest expense. We would spend hundreds of dollars on food a week. My mom and I tried to make everything from scratch, but feeding eight people on a very limited budget began to get cumbersome.

But God was already working behind the scenes to help us in this area. My sister told me about a food pantry supplied by health food stores only ten minutes down the road. They gave away organic foods that were usually only outdated by a day or two. I was so excited about this because I really loved eating healthy. Every Saturday morning, I was able to bring home twenty or more loaves of organic bread and some meat, eggs, and milk. Many times I raised my hands in humble adoration to God for His amazing provision in our lives. I couldn't believe God really cared about even the little things that mattered to me. I mean, who would have ever thought of a food pantry carrying organic healthy food?

Even with this amazing blessing, my dad was still spending quite a bit on our groceries. So while my parents were gone, I did some research and realized I might be able to get temporary government financial help that included free health care and food stamps. I wanted so desperately to avoid being a burden on my dad and mom that I decided to see if we qualified or not. After hours and hours of filling out paper work on each child, I was approved. Getting help like this was difficult for me because so many times I had heard through other Christians that government assistance is bad because people could end up being owned by the government. They felt the church should be the one to help single moms, orphans, and the widows, not the government.

Despite my uncertainty, I decided to go with the program. I was thrilled to learn that my two favorite grocery stores accepted food stamps. But, I was shamefully embarrassed when I went to the grocery store for the first time. I actually thought food stamps would be paper stamps you hand to the cashier. Thankfully it was like having a credit card. Before I pulled out the card, I looked around me to see if anyone was watching and hoped that the cashier would not say anything out loud about it.

One time just after we started using the stamps, the device that reads the card was down at the grocery store. When the cashier was finished scanning my groceries, she noticed I had a food stamp card. She yelled across the whole store, trying to get the managers attention, "I have a lady here who needs help with her food stamps!" I looked over at my oldest son and he was bright red. Everyone was staring at us and I wanted to run out of that store so fast. But, there I was with all five of my children. For a long time after that, Weston would stay in the car or at home because he did want to go grocery shopping with me. However, when I saw the benefits of getting public assistance far outweighed our embarrassment and pride, I was at peace. My dad no longer had to pay for any of our food and we now had free medical and dental.

In the meantime I was still attending my weekly life skills class. The church where the class was being held said that Adelynn could watch her brother and sisters in their nursery while I went to my class. This blessed me so much knowing that if there was an emergency, my kids were just down the hall.

That class was hugely instrumental in my healing process. I was very nervous and shy when I first started, but as the weeks progressed, I was gradually forced out of my comfort zone. I had to write out the events of my whole life from the time I was born until the present and then read it out loud to the whole class. This was grueling for me. Talking in front of people was already frightening, let alone sharing intimate details to women I barely knew. I remember calling my dad in Florida and jokingly asking him if he would present my timeline to the women instead of me. He laughed this time. But it wasn't very funny when I was in eighth grade and was asked to give the final speech at my graduation, but couldn't because I froze in fear. That time my dad actually got on stage and did my speech for me. However, this time God gave me the courage to tell my story. The more I read, the braver I became. It took over an hour to read, but I did it. I was able to face my pain, embrace it, and feel it, instead of feeling ashamed and hiding from it.

Writing out my story and learning so many crucial things about myself through the class was actually a turning point in my life. It brought an extensive healing to me and also helped me revisit and rehearse the timeline of my marriage. I not only began to see why Troy possibly reacted the way he did, but I also recognized the part I played in our dysfunction. With much sorrow, I realized the greatest way I could have honored and loved Troy was to confront his abuse. I should have cried out for help the first year of our marriage, not the fifteenth year. Regretfully, I had enabled the abuse, causing it to become a cancer that shamefully grew out of control.

Looking back now, I realize how foolish and prideful it was for me not to have called the police right away during the times that Troy's anger got out of control. I cowardly allowed the fear of my husband, my warped view of myself and what other people thought of us to control me, causing me to remain quiet.

If I had established healthy boundaries, a godly confidence in who I was as a wife and mother, a healthy view of what true submission and obedience in a marriage looks like, and trustworthy accountability partners surrounding us, our marriage might not have been so toxic.

I also saw how over the years, I began escaping my pain by focusing on the kids too much. I allowed the kids to come before Troy in our marriage, which resulted in me not being sensitive to his needs. I did not pursue my husband in a passionate, intimate way very often. Ashamedly, the more pain and unforgiveness I harbored, the less I wanted sex, which is probably why I blamed myself when I found out Troy was turning to pornography to get his needs met.

Honestly, I didn't grasp what a true help meet really was. I fully understand now that my calling as Troy's wife was to walk by his side as a humble companion of strength and power. This was not a power to lord over him but a beautiful, submissive, saving power uniquely created by God to specifically help Troy in the areas where he was weak.

> "Now the Lord God said, 'It is not good (beneficial) for the man to be alone; I will make him a helper [one who balances him—a counterpart who is] suitable and complementary for him'" (Gen. 2:18).

Wow! To not have realized when we got married that God specifically gave me a special grace no other woman had to help Troy prosper, succeed and fulfill God's call on his life as a man of God and effective leader he so desperately wanted to be, was heartbreaking. Instead, I unknowingly walked under Troy as someone to be controlled and commanded to obey, just like a child with her father. We had developed a very unhealthy codependency on each other. I remorsefully, got my confidence from what Troy thought of me instead of what God thought of me. This made me very insecure and "needy" at times. That neediness frustrated Troy, because it put a lot of unnecessary pressure on him as he tried to meet my deepest needs only God could meet. If only we had known and understood these concepts beforehand, then we probably would have seen and embraced each other as on the same team rather than always fighting against each other.

The bottom line was, my healing couldn't begin until my blaming ended. I could not try to "fix" Troy, change him, or blame him any longer! I was also not accountable for the things Troy did or the decisions he made. The best thing I could do for Troy and our marriage was to work on me and my problems. I had to let go of Troy and give him to God, fervently praying that He would do a miracle in Troy's life. My mandate was to become a whole person and to focus on becoming the beautiful woman, wife, and mommy God called me to be.

I cried out to God asking Him to forgive me for my part in hurting our relationship. Then I wrote Troy two letters. In the first letter, I asked him to forgive me for how I had hurt him over the years. I actually sent that letter to him, asking God to use it to bring healing to him. In the second letter, I wrote out the specific things Troy had done or said to me that deeply wounded me over the years. After reading it, I wept as I tore it up into what seemed like a thousand pieces, crying out loud, "I forgive you, Troy. I really do!"

Afterward I immediately felt such a huge burden lifted off of me, because in that moment I truly forgave Troy for every hurtful word and for every damaging action that he ever violated me with. In that moment of forgiveness, I had to give up the possibility of a better past. Even though I desperately wanted Troy to truly be sorry for his part in hurting his family, dejectedly he was not. But it no longer mattered to me because I was finally able to see Troy through the eyes of the cross. God even gave me a new and stronger compassion for Troy and a powerful grace to be able to let Troy go, trusting God with the outcome no matter what it might be.

This poem spoke volumes to me and helped me to differentiate the difference between whether I was really loving Troy or just trying to control him:

Let Go

To "Let Go" doesn't mean to stop caring,
It means I can't do it for someone else.
To "Let Go" is not to cut myself off,
It is the realization I can't control another.
To "Let Go" is not to enable,
But to allow learning from natural consequences.
To "Let Go" is to admit powerlessness,
Which means the outcome is not in my hands.
To "Let Go" is not to care for,
But to care about.
To "Let Go" is not fix,
But to support.

To "Let Go" is not to judge,
But to allow another to be a human being.
To "Let go" is not to be in the middle arranging all the outcome,
But to allow others to affect their own destinies.
To Let Go" is not to deny,
But to accept.
To "Let Go" is not to nag, scold or argue,
But instead to search out my own short comings and to correct them.
To "Let Go" is not to adjust everything to my desires,
But to take each day as it comes and to cherish them.
To "Let Go" is not to criticize and regulate anybody,
But to try to become what I dream I can be.
To "Let Go" is not to regret the past,
But to grow and to live for the future.
To "Let Go" is to fear less,
And to Love more. Author unknown

At this time I also felt like I needed to apologize to my children and my parents and ask them to forgive me for the many times I was defensive and reacted in frustration towards them. Even to this day, when I discipline in anger or frustration, my kids rebel and do not do what I tell them to do, or they obey with a bad attitude. However, when I apply what James 1:19-21 says and react calmly but firmly in a consistent, loving way, I am astounded to see with my own eyes the righteousness of God being produced in their life. As a result they want to please and obey me with a good attitude and a happy heart.

> "Understand this, my beloved brothers and sisters. Let everyone be quick to hear [be a careful, thoughtful listener], slow to speak [a speaker of carefully chosen words] and, slow to anger [patient, reflective, forgiving]; for the [resentful, deepseated] anger of man does not produce the righteousness of God [that standard of behavior which He requires from us]." James 1:19–21

With God helping me to apply His Words and the skills I learned in class to my life, I slowly began reacting in ways that were encouraging and healing. After six months of intense learning, I left the class with such clarity, boldness, hope and new found freedom. I was not a slave to unforgiveness, fear, and anger! The word "victim" was no longer in my vocabulary.

I felt like what Sleeping Beauty must have felt after her handsome prince kissed her and made her come back to life. Jesus graciously "kissed" me with His amazing love and forgiveness and caused me to wake up from the hopelessness and despair that had tormented me for so long. I was alive and free to finally live "happily ever after." I saw God's love and forgiveness in ways I never had before and was determined with God's grace, whether single or married, to live a life that was pleasing to Him.

CHAPTER 5
The Highest Career in the Nation

The more I read and studied the Bible, the more I realized that the greatest and most high-powered career in the nation for me was being a godly mother. It was such a humbling honor to know God entrusted me with five eternal beings. Since I did not have my husband with me, they were now my first ministry, my greatest calling, and my career.

Every time I tried to find a way to make an income or some type of a career without His help, God would remind me in the Scriptures that He was my employer! As long as I put Him first and taught my kids to know Him, then He promised me He would always provide for us:

> "Therefore, you shall impress these words of mine on your heart and on your soul, and tie them as a sign on your hand, and they shall be as bands (frontals, frontlets) on your forehead."

"You shall teach them [diligently] to your children [impressing God's precepts on their minds and penetrating their hearts with His truths], speaking of them when you sit in your house and when you walk along the road and when you lie down and when you rise up."

"You shall write them on the doorposts of your house and on your gates, so that your days and the days of your children may be multiplied in the land which the Lord swore to your fathers to give them, as long as the heavens are above the earth." Deuteronomy 11:18–21

Whenever I doubted or questioned my role as their mother, I would always try to remember when I gave birth to each child. Doing so would give me perspective and a vivid reminder of how much I really love them. I remember like it was yesterday when I first found out I was pregnant with my firstborn son. On January 17, 1996, I wrote the following in my journal:

Hallelujah! I am pregnant! According to the doctor, I am at sixteen weeks today. It is just a miraculous thing. I can't believe anyone would think there is no God. Troy is so excited. The first ultrasound we had was breathtaking. I was scared to death though. The doctor put the ultrasound wand on me and on the monitor we saw a heart beating really fast. It was so wonderful to look at Troy's face with so much joy and pride written all over it. I wish I had a camera. He went to every department at work and showed them the ultrasound pictures.

What I need to tell you is what happened when I first found out I had a little person growing in me. I went to Revco and bought a test, because I was one day late and I am never late. Then all the way home I kept telling myself "I am going to wait until Troy gets home to do this." But when I got home, joy just came over me and I lost all my patience. I ran upstairs, pulled out the little stick and went to the bathroom on it, praying the whole time. Then I had to wait ten minutes and those were the longest ten minutes ever.

Well, after I waited I went into the bathroom with anticipation, yet with a little hesitation. When I picked up the test, I screamed at the top of my lungs. It was positive! I wanted to call Troy, but he was at choir practice. So I ran downstairs and started writing him a little letter.

I got to "Dear Daddy" when all of a sudden I was overwhelmed with much joy and happiness. I fell on my knees and literally cried and thanked God for His mercy and grace. I was amazed and humbled that God would choose me to be a mommy! I finished the letter and when Troy got home, I ran outside on the porch and said, "Welcome home daddy." He said, "What?" I gave him the letter with the positive stick and after he read the letter, he was grinning from ear to ear.

To say the least, we are overjoyed about this beautiful, wise, smart, obedient, chosen, special, normal, every-part-intricately-wrought-by-God, loving, joyful, peaceful, giving, kind, patient, self-controlled, gentle, speaks-out-words-that-are-life-giving child of the most High King.

Except for Weston's birth, for which I had an epidural, I chose to birth each of my other four children naturally and without any pain medicine. I know that probably sounds crazy, but I had a really bad experience with the epidural I had with Weston, so I was determined to give it a try. At first it was very frightening and daunting to face the pain, especially knowing that once I decided to go medicine free, there would be no turning back. I had even read that the pain of birthing is similar to 20 bones getting fractured at one time. I was still determined with God's help to face my fear and go for it.

The coolest thing was, I don't think I was ever closer to God than when I was in the midst of my hardest labor. As the contractions got stronger and stronger, I became so vulnerable, so surrendered and so desperate that I had no choice but to cry out for my God to help me. The most powerful thing was that the more I cried out to Him and embraced my pain, the more God's peace and comfort surrounded me.

Whether I was giving birth in water or on a bed didn't matter. When I finally pushed that beautiful little head out, there was no greater reward for my hard labor than to bask in God's presence holding my precious baby, all the while praising God for His amazing love and grace. After every birth, God gave me a supernatural, fierce love for each child, an unconditional, selfless love. The neatest part about it all was when God showed me a beautiful glimpse of how Jesus must have felt and how much He loved us when He chose to bear the pain and suffer on the cross so we could be born again.

> "For God so [greatly] loved and dearly prized the world, that He [even] gave His [One and] only begotten Son, so that whoever believes and trusts in Him [as Savior] shall not perish, but have eternal life." John 3:16

> "Nicodemus said to Him, "How can a man be born when he is old? He cannot enter his mother's womb a second time and be born, can he?" Jesus answered, "I assure you and most solemnly say to you, unless one is born of water and the Spirit he cannot [ever] enter the kingdom of God" John 3:4-5

Whether you birth a child naturally (with or without medicine), by C-section, or by adoption doesn't matter, every child is a special, priceless gift from God. My mom and dad told me all the time that each one of my children was a representation of David's five smooth stones. My parents reminded me that David took five stones out of the brook to use to kill Goliath with his sling (1 Sam. 17:40). They told us over and over how special these children were and how much potential each one had and that each would one day be a stone who would triumphantly slay many giants.

I was extremely thankful for my parents' encouragement and beautiful perspective, especially during the times I most wanted to give up. I tried daily to look at my children as my calling and my ministry and not as a distraction trying to steal another, better calling away from me. The more I embraced and expected the good and the bad of this calling, the smoother my day would go. If at the end of the day taking care of them was all I accomplished, then at least I still knew God was pleased with me and that was all that mattered. I love this quote because it helped me realize how powerful my job as a mom really was.

"Your greatest contribution to the kingdom of God may not be something you do but someone you raise." Andy Stanley[3]

I wanted to be real with my children, even when it came to Santa Claus or the Tooth Fairy. I tried my best to always tell them the truth. If I lied in one area, how would they ever believe me in the areas that matter the most? I wanted them to internalize the things I was teaching them so with God's help they would actually understand it and most importantly live it!

I wanted them to have such a profound revelation of who God is, what He was telling them, and what I was telling them so that when I was away from them, they would still obey, not because they were forced to, but because they knew the reason why and therefore wanted to. "Obedience is like an umbrella. When you get out from under it, you get rained on." I would say quite often. I wanted them to understand how important it is to always obey God and the authorities He has placed in their life so they will continually be under God's umbrella of protection.

"Children, obey your parents in the Lord [that is, accept their guidance and discipline as His representatives], for this is right [for obedience teaches wisdom and self-discipline]."

"Honor [esteem, value as precious] your father and your mother [and be respectful to them]—this is the first commandment with a promise— so that it may be well with you, and that you may have a long life on the earth." Ephesians 6:1-3

Even when we were living in Florida, family reading time was one of our favorite things to do. It helped unite us together. We

3 Andy Stanley c 2013

really looked forward to it and tried to read at least once a week. This time taught the little ones to sit still and develop a greater attention span as well as fostering better reading comprehension. Some of our favorite books were the Bible and history, and we especially liked the refurbished children's books originally written in the1800s. I ended up having quite a collection of these old books. Because I loved them so much my friends and family got them for me for birthdays or Christmas. These stories were very well written. Many times after already reading a lot of chapters, my kids would yell, "Keep reading!" The vocabulary was extensive and the morals and Godly character addressed in the stories were life changing. As much as I loved reading out loud to the kids, it wasn't always easy. In the midst of trying to juggle everything as a single mom, there were many days I was too emotionally, physically and spiritually drained to do it. Many nights I would fall asleep beating myself up because we didn't have our special reading time together. Although, the times that we did get a chance to read together were very memorable and extra special.

Memorizing and meditating on Scripture and trying to apply it to our daily life were my first priorities. The atmosphere in our home would be more peaceful when we did these things.

"All Scripture is inspired by God and profitable for teaching, for reproof, for correction, for training in righteousness" (2 Tim. 3:16 NASB),

"Your word I have treasured and stored in my heart, That I may not sin against You" (Ps. 119:11).

Memorizing Scriptures through song seemed to be for us, the best way to do it. The kids would learn the verses fast and would sing them all the time. While homeschooling in Florida, I was elated to have found a cheap curriculum that took whole chapters in the Bible and put music to them. Over the years we were able to memorize quite a few chapters of the Bible with this method. Since we all really needed God's comfort while living at my parent's house, Psalm 91 became a chapter we loved and relied on all the time. Therefore, I decided this would be the chapter we would memorize. Anytime we were afraid and sang this Psalm, miraculously fear would leave us and a supernatural peace would embrace us. To know as a single mother that my children and I were safe and protected when we took refuge under the almighty wings of God was beyond comprehension. Every word continually brought hope and healing to our broken hearts. I can't even begin to count the times that I rocked Azaliah to sleep while singing Psalm 91 over and over to her.

After months of singing Psalm 91 before bed, in the middle of the night and in the mornings, we finally had all sixteen verses memorized. Even little Azaliah could sing a few of the words, although saying, "perilous pestilence" was nearly impossible at only eighteen months old.

One time Weston said, "Mom, did you know that Psalm 91 is called the Soldier's Prayer?" "No" I said. He told me the reason it was called the Soldier's Prayer is because soldiers prayed it all the time, asking God to protect them and help them to be brave in the middle of war. We all thought that was very cool, especially since to some degree we were in the midst of our own little war.

Psalm 91
He who dwells in the secret place of the Most High
Shall abide under the shadow of the Almighty.
I will say of the Lord, "He is my refuge and my fortress;
My God, in Him I will trust."
Surely He shall deliver you from the snare of the fowler,
And from the perilous pestilence.
He shall cover you with His feathers,
And under His wings you shall take refuge;
His truth shall be your shield and buckler.
You shall not be afraid of the terror by night,
Nor of the arrow that flies by day,
Nor of the pestilence that walks in darkness,
Nor of the destruction that lays waste at noonday.
A thousand may fall at your side,

And ten thousand at your right hand;
But it shall not come near you.
Only with your eyes shall you look,
And see the reward of the wicked.
Because you have made the Lord, who is my refuge,
Even the Most High, your dwelling place,
No evil shall befall you,
Nor shall any plague come near your dwelling;
For He shall give His angels charge over you,
To keep you in all your ways.
In their hands they shall bear you up,
Lest you dash your foot against a stone.
You shall tread upon the lion and the cobra,
The young lion and the serpent you shall trample underfoot.
"Because he has set his love upon Me,
therefore I will deliver him;
I will set him on high, because he has known My name.
He shall call upon Me, and I will answer him;
I will be with him in trouble;
I will deliver him and honor him.
With long life I will satisfy him,
And show him My salvation." (NKJV)

It was staggering for me to actually see with my own eyes how powerful the Bible really is. It was immensely reassuring to know that no matter what problem or sin we faced; somewhere in God's Word there would always be an answer for it.

"It is written and forever remains written, 'Man shall not live by bread alone, but by every word that comes out of the mouth of God.'" Matthew 4:4

Another area I had a passion for was to train my children to eat healthy. I wanted them to understand that their little bodies were specially created by God to be the temple or house of the Holy Spirit and how important it is to keep their "temple" in good working condition:

"Do you not know that your body is a temple of the Holy Spirit who is within you, whom you have [received as a gift] from God, and that you are not your own [property]?" (1 Corinthians 6:19).

When Weston was six weeks old, I found a lump the size of a small lemon on my neck. I was scared out of my wits, thinking I had cancer. Troy and I left Weston for the first time with close friends and immediately went to the emergency room. The doctor took a blood sample and said that my thyroid hormone levels were very low, I was almost ready to go into a coma. This explained why I had the lump, which was termed a goiter, on my neck. They diagnosed me with hypothyroidism, gave me Synthroid (a synthetic thyroid hormone) and told me to follow up with an endocrinologist.

A few weeks later I met with an endocrinologist and he said that I have Hashimoto's thyroiditis, an autoimmune disease that causes my own body to actually attack my thyroid and cause it to eventually stop secreting the thyroid hormone. He told me I would have to be on Synthroid for the rest of my life. I was not happy. I was only twenty-four years old at the time and I wanted desperately to refuse that diagnosis in my young life.

I also knew I didn't want the terrible symptoms Hashimoto's caused. My heart would race or skip a beat. I would get so cold that when I took a bath, I could have the water turned all the way hot and it wouldn't even phase me. I was tired and sluggish all the time, but I still couldn't sleep at night. Much of my hair fell out and I was very emotional and fearful about the littlest things. If Weston got sick, my first thoughts were that he was dying and many times I thought I was dying of some terminal illness. I consistently took the medicine for one full year and I was very grateful I did. Once the Synthroid got into my system, my thyroid shrank back to normal and all my other symptoms went away as well.

Even though the medicine was working and I felt back to normal, I didn't know the long term effects it would have on me or my future children. Therefore I really wanted to do whatever

I could to get off of Synthroid. First and foremost, Troy and I fervently prayed that God would heal me. I began searching different Scriptures on healing that proved to me that God really did want to heal me. When I took walks, drove in my van, did dishes, or went to sleep, I would listen to many of these healing Scriptures on tape, trying to exchange my fear with faith. Here are some of them:

"I will not die, but live, And declare the works and recount the illustrious acts of the Lord." Psalm 118:17

"My son, pay attention to my words and be willing to learn; Open your ears to my sayings. Do not let them escape from your sight; Keep them in the center of your heart. For they are life to those who find them, And healing and health to all their flesh." Proverbs 4:20–22

"Do not be wise in your own eyes; Fear the Lord [with reverent awe and obedience] and turn [entirely] away from evil. It will be health to your body [your marrow, your nerves, your sinews, your muscles—all your inner parts] And refreshment (physical well-being) to your bones." Proverbs 3:7–8

"Then a woman who had suffered from a hemorrhage for twelve years came up behind Him and touched the [tassel] fringe of His outer robe; for she had been saying to herself, "If I only touch His outer robe, I will be healed." But Jesus turning and seeing her said, "Take courage, daughter; your [personal trust and confident] faith [in Me] has made you well." And at once the woman was [completely] healed." Matthew 9:20–22

"But He was wounded for our transgressions, He was crushed for our wickedness [our sin, our injustice, our wrongdoing]; The punishment [required] for our well-being fell on Him, And by His stripes (wounds) we are healed." Isaiah 53:5

Eventually, God gave me an amazing faith, courage, and peace to trust Him for my healing. I no longer was afraid of my diagnosis.

"He will not fear bad news; His heart is steadfast, trusting [confidently relying on and believing] in the Lord" (Ps.112:7).

While I believed God would heal me, I also started doing extensive research on eating healthy and the effects that doing so would have on my body. My close friend Deena said she had started eating healthier and saw major results including not getting sick anymore, which escalated my motivation. The more research I did, the more I realized how God extraordinarily designed our bodies and if fed the right nutrition and kept in good physical condition, many times the body can actually heal itself. I began researching what foods nourished the thyroid and which were thyroid inhibitors. I also found out that stress was a huge contributing factor in developing a thyroid condition. Thus began my journey of eating healthy, exercising more frequently and learning to handle stress in a much more productive way.

After many months of praying, building up my immune system and gaining much faith and courage, I slowly started to wean myself off the Synthroid. However, I wasn't foolish. I went to the doctor to get my blood levels checked as much as possible. Every time I went in, my levels got better and better until eventually they were completely back to normal. After a while of doing this, I confessed to the doctor that I had not been on the Synthroid for many months and that I was trusting God and eating healthy instead. He was shocked when I told him this and said whatever I was doing was working and to keep doing it. He also said I no longer had to come back and see him anymore.

I walked out of that doctor's office with such a feeling of freedom from the bondage of having to take daily medicine and the constant piercing of my arm for blood draws. It was all miraculously over! I was vastly thankful to God for my healing and for the opportunity to be a witness to my doctor.

I had one flare up after my second pregnancy, but I have not had any thyroid issues since. I have been both medicine and symptom free for over seventeen years. God's Word really is true, and he is no respecter of persons. What He did for me He will do for anyone.

This experience was the main reason I was so passionate about teaching healthy eating to my children. Over the years my children have acquired a taste for healthy food and know why they eat the way they do, even if sometimes their friends don't. At first I was extreme about nutrition, but then God showed me that I was making it an idol in my life. He would remind me that He was our healer first and that eating healthy was just the fuel that helped our bodies work in tip-top condition. Overtime, especially as a single mom, I learned not to be overly strict about it. Especially since health food can be very expensive. We had "junk food" and candy every so often. If the kids went anywhere, they usually ate whatever was put before them. Thankfully, none of my kids were picky eaters.

As we continued to function as a single parent home, we had to learn a lot more about how to survive. I had to rely on my kids more than ever now, which was actually a blessing in disguise. We had to learn how to work together while we cleaned, made meals, and did laundry. The hardest part was getting along with one another in the process. I wanted the kids to take ownership of what was given to them.

I am not going to lie; keeping the house clean was very arduous for me. I enjoyed cooking but cleaning was not my gifting to begin with, let alone trying to keep up with so many little people in such a small space. I tried my best to make schedules and be consistent with them, but something always seemed to come up and thwart the schedule, causing me to become frustrated and overwhelmed.

A messy house really bothered Troy and it was one area I knew God wanted me to work on and become better at. My mom really helped me in this area. She was a very scheduled and organized person. She joyfully did laundry on Monday, ironing on Tuesday, mopping floors on Wednesday, grocery shopping on Thursday, vacuuming and dusting and cleaning bathrooms on Fridays, and tidying up the whole house on Saturdays. She did monthly chores like clean out the cars and the refrigerators, sweep and mop behind all the big appliances and wash all the windows and mirrors.

Mom was very consistent in everything she did. She had a beautiful servant's heart and was such an inspiration to me. Even though many times it was hard for me to meet her standards, overall it really helped us all to see how important it is to be good stewards of the things God gives us. Mom's example taught the kids the importance of hard work and serving others. My mom would always say, "Work before play." As we applied this principle to our lives, the kids enjoyed and appreciated their play time much more after they worked hard.

Looking back now, I highly appreciate these teaching times my mom gave, especially the memories we made together. She was my best friend and my very own prayer partner. She continually pointed me to Jesus and did not allow me to wallow in my despair. Without me realizing it, God was using her as a mentor and accountability partner in my life who inspired me to continue to become the godly mother and wife I so desperately wanted to be.

> "Older women similarly are to be reverent in their behavior, not malicious gossips nor addicted to much wine, teaching what is right and good, so that they may encourage the young women to tenderly love their husbands and their children, to be sensible, pure, makers of a home [where God is honored], good-natured, being subject to their own husbands, so that the word of God will not be dishonored." Titus 2:3–5:

The more I grew in my role as mother, the more I understood that many little eyes were watching me and many little people were following me and doing the things I did. The sobering fact was that my influence, wrong or right, could impact the eternal trajectory of each of my children. Therefore, I was passionate and determined to become more like Jesus every day.

This quote from Elisabeth Elliot is a profound and beautiful explanation that I read often to remind me what an honor and privilege mothering really is:

> *"The routines of housework and of mothering may be seen as a kind of death, and it is appropriate that they should be, for they offer the chance, day after day, to lay down one's life for others.*
>
> *Then they are no longer routines. By being done with love and offered up to God with praise, they are thereby hallowed as the vessels of the tabernacle were hallowed—not because they were different from other vessels in quality or function, but because they were offered to God.*
>
> *A mother's part in sustaining the life of her children and making it pleasant and comfortable is no triviality. It calls for self-sacrifice and humility but it is the route, as was the humiliation of Jesus, to glory."*[4]

---

4 Elizabeth Elliott, [Let me be a woman]

CHAPTER 6
Shepherding My Children's Hearts

After many weeks of doubting myself and a lot of outside criticism, I was finally settled and excited about homeschooling as a single mom. After all the turmoil in the past year, we hadn't done a lot of "school." I tried to teach while working nights at McDonalds but wasn't very successful with it. Therefore, I knew a few of the kids were a little behind on their academics, especially math. So my next priority was to try to get on top of my children's education.

As much as I tried, many days I still failed to find the time the energy, and the patience to teach each child separately. The more I tried to be like the school system and do it just like they did, the more frustrated I and my children became. The extreme pressure I put on them and myself to perform and compete with the "standard" of what was normal, the more in bondage I became. It affected Weston the most. I homeschooled him the first year as a seventh grader, but as an eighth grader he wanted to try school out. I called the closest Christian school just to see what our options were and they actually were able to give him a full ride scholarship. This was such an answer to prayer. Even though we all missed him, he really thrived and was able to meet special friends. He even joined a cheap fencing club the school offered that Weston paid for with money from his paper route job. When he got a job at Chic Fila at age fifteen he was able to splurge and buy a nice uniform.

As I prayed and sought God on how to teach the other children, He started showing me that the goal of homeschooling is not providing a rigorous education so the children would one day have a successful career. The goal is to know and seek God in all of who He is so they can apply what He teaches them to their own life on a daily basis. This approach would build strong character, life skills, wisdom, and discernment and would ultimately help the children succeed at anything God wanted them to pursue.

I wanted my children to grasp the fact that learning is not just something you do in school for six or seven hours a day and then you are finished until the next day. Learning is a lifelong process, a fun adventure every day, all day long, no matter what your age or what season of life you are in. I wanted them to always have a passion to learn new things. Most importantly, I wanted our school room to be full of freedom and love!

If you are reading this and your children go to a public or private school, please do not feel condemned. You have to do what God is showing you for your family. I believe many of these concepts can still be applied even if your children go to school every day. The goal is to help your child foster a love of learning and a desire to live God's Word, no matter what environment they are put in.

In the past I had done much research on the different ways of learning and I felt that for the time being, learning classically might be the best fit for us. Classical education is geared to a child's natural learning style and has been proven over time to be effective. Many great leaders and forefathers including C. S. Lewis, Thomas Jefferson, Sir Isaac Newton, and Aristotle are just a few of the many great thinkers who received a classical education. The neatest part about teaching this way was that I could teach all my children at the same time like they did in the past, teaching different grades all together in a one room school house.

When we lived in Florida, we attended a classical co-op that met once a week that we really enjoyed but we were only able to attend part of the year. The co-op used a curriculum founded on the Bible and each subject presented God as the Author and the Creator of that subject. The kids went to classrooms consisting of eight children who were their own age. There a tutor who was usually another homeschooling mother or father presented everything they needed to memorize and learn for the rest of the week in history, science, Latin, geography, English grammar, math, timeline, and the Bible.

At home I would then teach my children all together as if we were in our own little one room school house. Once they were ten years old, we added to our studies intense English, writing, and math courses. The only subjects they had to do individually before they were ten were phonics and handwriting.

I loved this method because it gave me accountability and gave the kids a fun way to be in a classroom setting and meet new friends once a week. If the program ever got too intense for any of my children, I had the freedom to modify it to that child's level. The best part was, we could be completely done with school in only two or three hours. I was strict on reading because I believed a whole new world would open up to them if they had a love of reading. So every day they had quiet time to read.

Many times if the kids wanted to see a movie and the movie happened to be made from a book, they would have to read the book first and as a reward they could later watch the movie. It was so rewarding for me to see the kids read the *Chronicles of Narnia* series, the *Little House on the Prairie* series, the *Lord of the Rings* trilogy, *Because of Winn Dixie*, and many other books before they could watch the corresponding movies. The greatest thing was that they usually ended up telling me the books were way better.

I thought it would be amazing if there was a classical home-school co-op in Ohio near where my parents lived. I decided to call HSLDA (Homeschool Legal Defense Association), which always had a wealth of information and ask if they knew of any classical co-ops in my area. They said there were many around my area and the closest one was about fifteen minutes away. They gave me the name of the director, Rachel, who ironically only lived a few minutes down the road.

I was excited. I called Rachel and over time we developed a sweet friendship. Her children and mine were all about the same ages and she and her husband were such a great support for me. I ended up becoming a tutor for her co-op and was able to get paid. What I made offset the tuition for my children, so I didn't have to pay for their co-op instruction and I ended up with a little money left over. However, all the different curriculum materials were very expensive and I did not have enough money to buy everything my kids needed.

As I was thinking and praying about my situation, I vaguely remembered the conversation I had with HSLDA. During that phone call, they mentioned a scholarship they offer for single moms who are trying to homeschool. They said that I qualified but I would need to send in my story and they would choose the winner. I called back and asked them to send me the information. At the last minute I submitted my story and then waited for what seemed like an eternity. Just a few weeks later I received a letter in the mail from them. I anxiously opened it up, and a huge check for $2,000 fell to the ground! The card was so beautifully written, encouraging me and letting me know that they were praying for us.

I immediately danced around the whole house waving that check in the air and praising God for His provision. I ran to show the kids, as I wanted them to witness how God was truly being our provider! I couldn't believe that God provided the money for the kids' curriculum and also the tutoring job which provided me a beautiful way to make money with my children right beside me.

I eventually met a wonderful gal who also went to the co-op. She asked me if I wanted to work as a receptionist for a local nursing home. The hours were in the evenings. After thinking and praying about it, I decided to take the job. I could homeschool during the day and the kids would only be alone in the evenings for about four or five hours at a time. After I saw how much stress my parents were under when I was working nights at McDonalds, I decided from then on whenever I made a decision, I would try to always make it as if I was living completely on my own, without having to rely on my parents. I only wanted to use my parents if there was an emergency. This way they could have the freedom to leave for a vacation or go out on dates and not feel tied down having to babysit the kids. This also prepared my kids and me for the future, if and when we would ever have to move out and live on our own. Adelynn was becoming a very good and responsible babysitter and her younger siblings really listened to her.

My parents graciously let us use a part of their finished basement as a classroom. They let us use their book shelves, and Dad even hung a huge white board up on the wall so I could write things down. Only with God's grace and mercy did we continue trying to embrace our situation and live each day to the fullest. Over time I began to have more motivation to get out of the house and do fun things.

As homeschoolers, field trips were one of our favorite things to do. We would get together with our special friends and have fun learning together. These trips would help us to see in real life the things we were learning in our curriculum. However, since I was on a very limited budget, I had to intentionally look for things to do that were free or cheap. Paying admission for five children really adds up.

As I did my research, I couldn't believe the different learning things our community offered. The local parks and recreation was one of my favorite resources. They had toddler days, preschool days and even homeschooling days, all for free. Through our community, my kids were able to wade in rivers while being taught all the different creatures, algae, and mosses. They got to go on lightening bug hikes at sunset and learn how to milk a cow, take care of a farm, grow a garden, cook food on an indoor fire, watch animals in their natural habitat, make candles, live like a pioneer, see a live Civil War battle reenactment, hike through caves and learn about bats and stalactites and stalagmites, find fossils, swim in a lake and so much more. Weston even got to learn how to fly a real little airplane.

My parents bought a zoo membership one year and a creation museum membership the next year for our Christmas present. These memberships were another tremendous help on our journey of learning together as a family. I was also able to find all five kids quality and free swimming lessons every year from Ohio State University. Each child learned to be an excellent swimmer because of this program.

Homeschooling was very difficult at times, especially when things happened unexpectedly. On one autumn day, we had just gotten home from a field trip to an observatory that taught us all about the stars, the sun, and the sky. I wanted the older kids to do some chores, so I told Adelynn to go do the dishes and Dalton to vacuum out the car. After Adelynn was finished, she headed outside to help Dalton. This is her take on what happened that day.

After I did the dishes, I went outside to help my brother, who was seven, vacuum the car out. Now let me rewind a little bit because earlier that morning I'd been so excited to go to the observatory that I had dressed up in a white ruffled shirt with a cute little jumper and some little high-heel sandals. I was still wearing these when I went outside to help my brother.

When I got out there, he teased me to the point where I was very peeved. One of the things that made me kind of cringe with annoyance was that he was standing right next to a plug and then asked me to plug the vacuum in for him. I of course laughed and said no I don't think so, and he replied with a snooty yes you have to.

I then squealed and ran around the corner to the back of the house where I climbed up my favorite climbing tree. This special tree was where I went every single day to converse my thoughts with God and to be alone.

What started out as a chore ended up being a childish game of tag. I climbed higher and higher and higher and my brother started climbing up after me. I then tried to go climb back down on the other side of the tree (mind you, I was still in my heels and dress). Anyway my shoe slipped on a branch and I fell tumbling down about eight feet to the ground. I found out later that I hit my arm on a tree root that was sticking out of the ground and my back on plastic tubing around the tree. When I landed I got knocked out of breath and was frantically grasping for air. Dalton jumped out of the tree, ran down beside me and asked if I was okay. I gasped, "No," and then I blacked out.

Dalton went inside and told mom who then ran out back. By the time she got out there, I'd woken up and started walking towards her. She told me later that I looked as pale as a ghost, maybe even paler and my arm was swinging limply at a crazy angle by my side.

Mom immediately put me in the car and drove me to the children's hospital that was about ten minutes away. When I first awoke after my black out, my arm didn't hurt. It simply felt dislocated, but then on the way to the hospital it started throbbing. I realized then that my arm was broken and I started chanting aloud, "I broke my arm, I broke my arm." By the time we got to the hospital, I was in intense pain.

A kind elderly woman came out to the car with a wheelchair and settled me into it without causing me too much pain. We went into the hospital and I got accepted immediately into the back room where they take x-rays. It was intense! After that a beautiful, kind African-American nurse named Angel temporarily bandaged up my arm. She kept telling me I was such a sweet and brave little girl and that I deserved a stuffed animal.

Now when she said stuffed animal, I was immediately faced with visions of movies I had watched where the doctors had given their young patients cheap $1.00 animals from the dollar store. That was

63

not the case with me. She came back with an adorable stuffed teddy bear whom I immediately fell in love with and proudly christened with the name Snowball. (I found out later it was from the Columbus Zoo and Aquarium and was worth $17.00). Angel quietly told me and my mom that my arm was broken so badly that I would have to be transported by ambulance to the Nationwide Children's hospital in downtown Columbus, Ohio.

The more I conversed with this special nurse named Angel, the more I believed she was an actual angel! First, because of her name, second, because who gives a child you have never seen before a $17.00 bear? Especially when stuffed animals were my favorite gift. Third, because she bandaged up my arm in such a way that I didn't feel any pain and she comforted me and prayed over me that I would not feel any pain the whole ride to the hospital. And fourth, because my mom and I felt an overwhelming sense of peace.

But when I got to the hospital in Columbus, things started getting worse by the moment. I stood to get out of my wheelchair. I felt dizzy and faint and I couldn't see straight. A nurse then got me into bed and that was when the pain escalated. I was in pain the whole night. But thankfully my mom was right beside me and there was an amazing, sweet nurse named Sarah, if I remember correctly, who stayed up all night, making sure I was as comfortable as I could be. I found out that I had to have surgery to put a metal rod in because I broke my arm in two places at my elbow. I broke my wrist too.

I remember when they rolled me into surgery and started giving me the knock out gas. The anesthesiologist kept asking about my siblings and about my family, then I blacked out. When I finally awoke for good, it was 5:00 p.m. My mom got me a little toy from the store in the hospital, and I told her I wanted to go home. So we checked out and went home. I called my brothers up the night before to ask what color cast I should get. They both said I should get army green camouflage, but I got neon pink instead. The recovery took about eight weeks in total.

That time in the hospital with Adelynn was painfully lonely. Thankfully my mom and dad were watching the other kids, but there I was having to handle such major decisions all on my own. Watching my daughter in such agony was more than I could bear. To think that she would have to be put to sleep to have surgery and that we would have to stay the night together, alone in a hospital, was frightening to me.

After I got Adelynn comfortable and at peace, I went down to the public computers and sent Troy an email. My heart was hurting intensely. I could barely see the computer keyboard because of the tears flooding my eyes. I texted Troy and sent him an email telling him what happened to Adelynn. Deep down I desperately wanted him to fly to Ohio. I longed for him to come and comfort his daughter.

As I walked those hospital floors and rode on the many elevators back to Adelynn's room, there were people surrounding me everywhere. Yet, I still felt completely and utterly alone.

Troy never did come. After Adelynn was safely home I could finally relax and gather all my thoughts. I was amazed at how much God and His favor really were with us the whole time. I was very thankful for the sweet nurse named Angel who I really believe God strategically placed in our life, at the right place and at the right time. She saw something special in Adelynn. God's protection was definitely on Adelynn because her fall could have been much worse.

My church and homeschool family covered us in prayer and visited us, bringing a meal and a gift for Adelynn. Thankfully, the metal rod eventually came out and Adelynn's arm never suffered any complications after that. The whole procedure ended up being completely free since I was on government insurance. This was another situation through which God taught me to be courageous and overcome my fears even when I felt like no one was by my side.

> "Be strong and courageous, do not be afraid or tremble in dread before them, for it is the Lord your God who goes with you. He will not fail you or abandon you."
> Deuteronomy 31:6

But most importantly, what we went through was a tangible life event that reiterated and confirmed to my kids that schooling at home wasn't just book learning. It was also learning how to handle surprise emergencies in life in a gracious, fearless way, trusting God with an attitude of giving Him all the glory. This huge and necessary life skill would be used again and again for the rest of their lives.

The honor of really being able to teach my children at home and overcome huge obstacles and setbacks in the process was another overwhelming confirmation that God was my provider. He was teaching me to trust Him in my calling and journey as a homeschooling, single mother every step of the way!

> "Roll your works upon the Lord [commit and trust them wholly to Him; He will cause your thoughts to become agreeable to His will, and] so shall your plans be established and succeed." Proverbs 16:3

PART II
THE DEATH

"Not everything that is faced can be changed,
but nothing can be changed until it is faced"

-James Baldwin

CHAPTER 7
The Day My Dream Died

It was already summer time, over one year since we left Florida and the kids had still not seen their dad. They were beyond excited when Troy started communicating with them again. Weston bought a webcam for the laptop with his own money that he earned from his paper route in the hope that Troy would Skype him. The kids were mesmerized and fascinated by seeing their dad for the first time, "live" in over a year. It tore me up to see Weston taking the laptop all over the house to show Troy where they slept, where they ate and their special homeschooling room in the basement. Weston even showed him all the many Lego creations he had built. They would talk a few times a week and the older kids would actually play board games with their dad through the computer.

During one of the Skype calls, Troy told the kids that he was coming to visit. They were exhilarated. We marked the date on our calendars and counted down the days. He was coming in July, which happened to be the time of Azaliah's second birthday. Troy never really got to bond with her as much as the others, so

I thought it would be a neat time for him to come and celebrate her precious life.

Yet again, he never showed up. This was another blow to the kids' already broken hearts. They continued talking via Skype, but I began to notice they were not as enthused about it as before. Many times I found Audrynn, who was five years old, actually sitting on the keyboard with her face close to the screen while she was talking to Troy. I asked her why she did that and she said, "I am trying to sit on daddy's lap." Hearing that just broke my heart.

I could tell Weston and Adelynn were starting to lose hope that they would ever see their dad again. In fact, it got to the point where I had to tell Troy that until he came to visit them in person, the kids could no longer Skype him. I told him I didn't mind him talking to the kids on the phone, through email, or through letters and gifts, but Skyping them was too tormenting for them. It made them miss him so much more, and I could tell they were regressing emotionally in many ways.

As I was tucking Azaliah in bed one night, at only two and a half years old, she looked up at me and said so clearly, "You know that man in Texas? He's my dad and he is lost." What she said brought me to tears. It was so simple yet so profound and was the only way a two year old could reason in her little mind where her daddy was. He was lost.

Adelynn began complaining of stomach aches on a regular basis. I had to force her out of her room to do something fun. Azaliah kept waking up throughout the night, as if she was scared. Weston had a lot of frustration and Audrynn started sucking her two fingers again, like she did when she was a baby. Dalton actually woke up one night from a nightmare about his daddy and he cried a lot more. He longed for his daddy to play with him.

Troy was not happy about my decision to allow no more Skype calls. He began telling highly respected people we knew, our former pastor and friends, that I was purposely keeping the kids away from him and turning them against him. This was so hurtful to me. I wanted to try to defend myself many times until

I finally resolved to just trust that God would defend me and the truth would prevail.

"The Lord will fight for you while you [only need to] keep silent and remain calm." Exodus 14:14

Through all of this I could tell that the kids could use some outside counseling. After a lot of searching, I was able to find a Christian counselor who helped low income families. All the children except Weston went to see her. Even though they didn't enjoy it too much, I believe it really helped them to be able to express how they were feeling and it gave them creative tools to help them process everything. They went for about six weeks, and then the counselor felt they were solid and secure about things.

What was so tormenting about my situation was the fact that I really was a widow in every sense of the word. My kids did not see their dad every other weekend or seven days on and seven days off. I had them twenty-four a hours a day, seven days a week for already over a year. We still had not gotten any money or support from him in any way.

Knowing my husband was dead would probably have been so much easier to deal with. At least we would have had the finality of knowing there was no chance he would ever come back. Knowing that he was still alive and out there somewhere created a mourning that never seemed to end. We daily hoped that one day he would be changed and come rescue us, love us and fight for us so we would be a family again.

I have always believed that any marriage can be saved and restored, even in cases of adultery and abuse, as long as both parties are truly sorry for what they did wrong and prove they will never do it again. But abandonment seemed impossible to reconcile. Through every situation, God continued to give me the strength. I prayed constantly for the reassurance of knowing that God really is my husband, my judge and my protector and He would be the Father to my kids they so desperately wanted to have.

"A father of the fatherless and a judge and protector of the widows, Is God in His holy habitation." Psalm 68:5

I knew forgiving Troy was the only way I could ever truly heal and become the woman God called me to be. I had already forgiven him when I went to my class the year before. But I wanted to make sure I was walking in forgiveness on a daily basis. Forgiveness is not just a one-time occurrence but an ongoing process. I wanted my children to always walk in forgiveness towards their father and their best teacher was me, trying with God's help to model forgiveness in front of them.

> As Jesus said, "For if you forgive others their trespasses [their reckless and willful sins], your heavenly Father will also forgive you" (Matt. 6:14),

> "Whenever you stand praying, if you have anything against anyone, forgive him [drop the issue, let it go], so that your Father who is in heaven will also forgive you your transgressions and wrongdoings [against Him and others]" (Mark 11:25).

However, forgiving someone who still wasn't sorry for his part was overwhelming and extremely difficult for me to do. The anger I felt was like a destructive tool drilling down and piercing the deepest parts of my heart, pulling out and then doing it over again and again. It was getting harder and harder for me to forgive Troy on a daily basis. The times I did talk to or email him, I would react in such pitiful ways, begging him to please send money and come see his kids or at least just give us a good reason of why he wasn't able to.

Even if I was the worst wife in the world, the kids still desperately need you as their dad. Abandon me all you want, but please don't abandon your kids, I cried out in anguish.

The more I reacted to his actions and words in negative ways, the more I realized he was still controlling me even from hundreds of miles away. I was the one to blame, not him. I was allowing him to control my thoughts, will and emotions.

I prayed the Scripture Malachi 4:6 so many times, longing for Troy's heart to be turned back to his kids:

"He will turn the hearts of the fathers to their children, and the hearts of the children to their fathers [a reconciliation produced by repentance], so that I will not come and strike the land with a curse [of complete destruction]."

Deep down I knew it was time to pursue legal action, but it took some time of fervently praying and talking with my parents. I talked to different pastors and many godly friends to get their opinions on what I should do before I took action. I also wanted to give Troy a last ditched effort to see if he would fight for his family, send money and visit us on his own initiative out of love and not because he was forced. It was a painful and extremely difficult process, but little by little with God's powerful grace I started to walk again in forgiveness towards my husband. Paul's story in 2 Corinthians 12:9 was encouraging to me. To know that God was really infusing me with the perfect amount of grace and power to help me forgive Troy on a daily basis was amazing:

"My grace is sufficient for you [My lovingkindness and My mercy are more than enough—always available—regardless of the situation]; for [My] power is being perfected [and is completed and shows itself most effectively] in [your] weakness." Therefore, I will all the more gladly boast in my weaknesses, so that the power of Christ [may completely enfold me and] may dwell in me.

However dealing with so many heartbreaks, Troy not sending any money and not even telling us his new address, or where he worked, was exasperating. Especially since we found out that he did indeed have a job and was living in an apartment on his own. Seeing no hope or plan of restoration and reconciliation, started to take a toll on us all. We were physically, emotionally and spiritually not able to stand the hopeless situation any longer. After much prayer, heartache, and counsel, I finally came to the realization that true forgiveness doesn't mean I should keep allowing Troy to hurt us. It was time to stop reacting to him and to start responding to him with tough love. I believed the best and only way to do that was to put up some healthy boundaries.

I wrote Troy an email and told him I was going to have to take legal action if he continued to refuse to pay child support and not come visit. I typed it and retyped it, praying that I would say exactly what God wanted me to say. I was so relieved when Troy emailed me a few weeks later saying that he was coming to visit in October for Audrynn's sixth birthday. At the same time I was so frustrated because he never mentioned anything about me pursuing legal action. We were very apprehensive about it, but all the while hoped he would come for sure.

It was true. After sixteen months of the kids not seeing Troy, he finally came! I surprised the kids. I took them to the airport telling them we were taking a tour, which we did. We went to all the different shops and saw the different airlines. Audrynn and Azaliah were mesmerized by the huge escalators.

After we were finished with the tour, I took them to where Troy's plane would be landing. Thankfully, Troy had already landed and was sitting in the waiting area. I told the kids, "That man looks familiar. I wonder who he could be?" They immediately started screaming and ran to give their daddy a huge hug. It was a beautiful sight. The past sixteen months of not seeing their dad did not change their view of him. They loved and embraced him with such an innocent, pure, unconditional love that only God could enable them to give.

Troy assumed he was staying with us because he didn't make any other arrangements. Even though it was very awkward and extremely hard for my parents and me, we allowed Troy to stay in the basement with the boys. My mom even gave him a hug when he walked through the door. We were all hoping that we would see a difference in him. We tried to walk in forgiveness towards him, but the more we conversed with him, the more we realized he was still walking in complete denial of everything. He still never mentioned my email about pursuing legal action.

I waited a few days and then I brought it up to him. My mom watched the kids while we talked and it did not end well. I was angry with him. As the days passed the angrier I became. He was still not sorry for his abandonment. In fact, he talked to me, the kids, and even my parents as if nothing had ever happened. He was nice but still very coy and evasive, refusing to tell us anything about himself. He did not give me or my parents any thanks or money for the sixteen months we sacrificed so hard to provide for our children.

What hurt the worst was noticing that he no longer wore his wedding ring. I asked him about it and he said he had to take it off for his work and accidentally lost it. I was devastated. I wore my ring faithfully as a statement of faith that our marriage would be saved.

After he left, I had a greater peace and confidence in my plan of pursuing child support. Troy did not contact us for many months after he left. Adelynn's birthday and Thanksgiving came and went without any communication from him.

It was now Christmas, the kids second Christmas without their daddy with them. We still hadn't heard from Troy and I didn't have any money to buy presents for the kids. The hardest part was the battle I was going through of whether or not I should set a date for a court hearing. It was continually lingering in my mind and causing me to be distracted quite often. God relentlessly kept showing His unfailing love and favor towards me, my parents and the kids. I couldn't believe how the church family stepped up and helped my family. I stood in awe of His amazing provision and all from different sources.

My brother David and his wife, Angelia sent all five of my kids much needed warm winter coats with hats and gloves. Another church heard my story and sent a $950 check to me and the church we were attending adopted my kids for Christmas and bought them quite a few gifts. My friend Patricia gave me a cell phone and told me she would pay for it for as long as I needed it. This was a huge answer to prayer and a tremendous relief. I was overwhelmed with thankfulness every time I used it.

A special woman, Shelley, whom I babysat for when I was a young girl, was now married, and was such an encouragement in my life. She was like another little sister to me. She paid for many counseling sessions for me with a Christian woman she highly recommended. She also bought our whole family a yearly membership to our local science museum that the kids loved to go to.

Our best friends from Florida came and visited! It was such a fun and perfect gift to have my closest friend Gina and all her kids with us to celebrate Jesus' birthday together. This got our mind off everything and gave my kids the best present in the world, their presence. Gina is such an immovable strength in my life. So many times I would call her on the phone crying to her about my situation and she would always have a beautiful word of encouragement or life changing prayer for me, that would help me make it through the day.

Another gift arrived on Christmas Eve when the doorbell rang and I happened to be the one who answered it. To my surprise no one was there, only a huge glass jar full of money. It had a little Christmas card taped on top and a big red bow tied around it! I picked it up and yelled to the kids to come. Their eyes were mesmerized looking at all the money in the jar. There were pennies, nickels, dimes, quarters, and a lot of paper money. It filled the jar to the very rim. We read the card attached: "May the God of hope fill you with all joy and peace as you trust in him, so that you may overflow with hope by the power of the Holy Spirit." Romans 15:13 NIV

By far the jar of money was my favorite gift. I felt like God Himself put it on our porch that night. He wanted to show me in a creative way that He will always provide for us like He promised He would. We emptied the jar and counted every last penny with such joy and a lot of laughter. Even little Azaliah joined in and tried to count. We ended up counting about $400.

I still have that little card and jar as a memorial and constant reminder from God that He will provide and will always give me hope, just as He promised.

After Christmas was over and things settled down a little, I decided to search for any options, resources, and law firms that could help me in my situation. After only a few weeks, I was excited to find a legal aid society, a government agency that helps low income families get child support at a reduced cost, as long as the situation was "no contest." After giving them all my information and attending a few of their meetings, they said I definitely qualified. The lawyer told me they found Troy's address in Texas and the fast food restaurant where he was working. My lawyer subpoenaed Troy's employer to see how much money he made.

I was amazed how fast my lawyer was able to get child support coming in. The court gave me temporary full custody of the children until the final hearing. Troy's employer would automatically take money out of his paycheck every two weeks. Although he was only making a little more than minimum wage and the support was very small, I was so thankful to have anything that would help my parents and me provide for our children.

The final hearing was fast approaching. I felt forced between two options, legal separation or divorce. This decision was the most painful choice I ever had to make.

During this time of seeking, I strongly felt I should contact a few of Troy's friends and acquaintances I knew who were still in contact with him. It was one thing to get advice from people who only knew my side of the story, but to get advice from people who knew Troy and his side of the story was something I felt I really needed to do. I knew that if they gave any inkling Troy was a changed person and they could see hope, then I would keep fighting for reconciliation.

The two I talked to, one being his closest friend, said that they had not heard from him in a long time and he had broken all ties with them. Another who was a recent counselor of Troy's. He told me Troy had stopped coming to him for counsel or advice and by what he could tell in their past communication, Troy was not changed. Since Troy had not sent us any support or visited for over a year, then he really felt Troy fit the description of 1 Timothy 5:8: "If anyone fails to provide for his own, and especially for those of his own family, he has denied the faith [by disregarding its precepts] and is worse than an unbeliever [who fulfills his obligation in these matters]." This really gave me a wake-up call. Even Troy's own friends were telling me that Troy did not want to fight for us. I hated to admit it, but it seemed to me that Troy's heart was beginning to harden.

I had always believed God hates divorce so much that he might even hate the person who was divorced. I also felt that if I divorced my husband, then I lied to God when I said my vows on my wedding day. So, I had this tormenting mind battle going on, thinking God and my children would hate me and that I would be labeled a liar for the rest of my life. Because of this, I decided to legally separate. That way I could still be married but have all the benefits of having full custody and child support.

The sheriff sent the papers to Troy's work and to his apartment requesting him to come to the court hearing so he could agree or disagree. Sorrowfully, there was no response. So many days I cried out to God to help heal my broken heart. I thought for sure pursuing legal action would help Troy turn from his ways and come fight for us. I was so distraught that he did not respond that I decided at the last minute to cancel the court hearing. Thankfully, my lawyer gave me a few more months before we had to decide on anything and have the final hearing.

In many of my journal entries, I cried out to God to save my marriage, begging God to forgive me if I had said or done anything that was contrary to His Word or against Troy. I asked Him to help me be a better mom. I continued to pray for Troy and our children, pleading with God to heal all of their hurts. I wanted God to renew a right spirit in me. I did not want any pride or fear to rule any of my decisions. I desperately needed His presence, wisdom, favor and strength in everything I did. More than anything I wanted to not just know the Bible, I wanted live it on a daily basis.

"Create in me a clean heart, O God, and renew a steadfast spirit within me. Do not cast me away from your presence and do not take you Holy Spirit from me." Psalms 51:10-11

After months of not hearing from Troy, I finally got a call on my cell phone from him. This was rare. When he did call it was usually to my parents' home phone. I actually got excited. I thought this call might be the one in which he would say something like, "God has really been dealing with me about things and I see where I have abandoned my family. I want to come fight for you. I will do whatever it takes to win my family back."

Sadly he did not say this. He asked to talk to the kids instead of me. I let him talk to them. Adelynn went first. I overheard her talking and knew the conversation was not going the way I thought it would. After they hung up, Adelynn said to me in tears, "Daddy said he is homeless and hungry and the reason why is because you, Mommy, are taking all of his money." She proceeded to tell me I needed to stop taking money out of his paycheck so he could find a home to live in and food to eat.

This hurt me more than words could say, because he used his own eleven-year-old daughter as a manipulative tool to make us feel sorry for him. This was a stab to the heart that hurt like no other. Here I had been raising our five children for eighteen months and he had not sent one penny and had only came to visit one time. He had the audacity to try to hurt his own daughter and turn her against me. It was more than I could handle.

I had an emotional melt down. All the kids and my parents heard me. Weston who was fourteen at the time came up to me and tried so hard to comfort me. He said, "Mom, it's okay. Actually to some degree, we are the ones who are homeless." This really made me see that he definitely saw the whole picture.

Most importantly though, Adelynn realized Weston was right. We were without a home to call our own too. Their dad providing for them should take precedent over anything else.

My parents sat the kids all down and reiterated to them how a father's first priority should be to take care of his family. They told them I was not doing anything wrong by asking their dad for money so I could have help in raising them. They told the kids that they didn't have to worry about their dad being homeless or hungry because God would take care of him.

79

I continued to take my marriage very seriously and extensively read and studied many different Scriptures on marriage, separation, and divorce. I again talked to a few pastors and their wives about my situation and asked for their godly opinions, prayer and advice.

I listened intently to everyone. However, through all of this I had to ask myself, "What is God telling me to do?" If I didn't know beyond any doubt what God and His word was telling me, then I knew I would always regret my decision. During this time of intense prayer and reflection, God showed me a passage of scripture that spoke volumes to me. Over the years I have read I Corinthians 7 many times because it talked intensely on marriage but this time I saw verse 17 in a new and profound way.

> "Only, let each one live the life which the Lord has assigned him, and to which God has called him [for each person is unique and is accountable for his choices and conduct, let him walk in this way]. This is the rule I make in all the churches." I Corinthians 7:17

This verse boldly declared to me that no matter what state our marriage was in, it didn't matter. I knew God could heal and restore the worst of the worst. Therefore, I had to resolve in my heart the only thing that mattered was what God was telling me to do.

After much prayer and a wholesome fear of displeasing God, I called my lawyer and told him I decided to legally divorce. The sheriff's department in Texas again gave papers to Troy, but we did not hear a word from him.

Many of you may stop reading this and never pick this book up again because you disagree with my decision. Or you might be in the midst of a failing marriage and God is telling you differently. He is telling you to keep fighting, keep pursuing, keep trusting God as you stay married. I want to strongly encourage you to keep on keeping on. Don't give up. If you are doing what God told you to do, then I know He will restore your marriage in the most glorious way. Seek God with all your heart, because He will direct your paths.

May 17, 2011 almost two years after the date we left Florida, was a day I will never forget. It was our final court hearing. I asked my dad and my close friend Patti, who was a huge support, to go with me. Her beautiful perspective on life and her selfless, giving heart and my dad's unconditional love were such a comfort to me. As much as I wanted my mom there too, she graciously watched all the kids for me.

I am so glad Dad and Patti were with me, because when I walked in that court room, it seemed very eerie, cold, and abnormally big. Patti gave me a beautiful encouraging card and she and my dad prayed for me before I stood in front of the judge. I was still fervently praying Troy would show up. I even glanced back at the door a few times, hoping I would see him. Sadly, he did not show up. I dejectedly went up and nervously stood before the judge. She gave me full custody of all the kids and said Troy needed to see the kids once a month in Ohio, with no sleep overs, since it had been more than six months since he had last visited.

The whole process lasted less than ten minutes and cost only about $150 dollars. It was heartbreaking and devastating to me that something so life altering could be finalized so cheaply and so quickly.

May 17, 2011

Well, it is final. I am divorced. I can't believe I am actually going through this horrendous tragedy. I feel like history has tragically been rewritten and my children's heritage has been adversely affected. I stand numb to it all. God, I bear my soul to you. As of right now, I think I hate myself. In the natural I am a hopeless mess. I am devastated that the dream I longed for my whole life has died.

Please help me to see that being a wife does not define who I am. But God, what does define me? Who am I? I feel so old and wrinkled, with nothing to offer this world. God please help me see myself the way You see me and help me to forgive myself and to receive Your unmerited grace. I desperately need You to teach me how to love myself as a divorced person. I need to embrace Your love for me. Help me to see that Your love will cast out all my fear and anger and any title that I am now given.

CHAPTER 8
Naked But Not Ashamed

During this rough time of grieving my divorce, I found out who my true friends really were. Whether it was in the homeschooling circles, with old acquaintances, in Bible studies, or in different churches we would visit, when people found out about my situation, they would sometimes say things like, "I don't know how you do it all," or "You sure do have your hands full." *I do it all because I have to,* I would think. *I don't have a choice.*

I even felt like some people thought I had committed the unpardonable sin and therefore no longer wanted to be associated with me. Some people even "threw" money at me, thanking God they weren't the ones wearing my shoes. I hated the pity. I would leave their presence feeling ashamed, judged and hopeless, thinking I had no way out. As I battled all these emotions, God began to teach me the difference between sympathy and compassion.

He showed me that sympathy is feeling sorry for the person, pitying them from a distance, causing the person to remain in their victimized state. Compassion is when you suffer alongside someone. It is when you see greatness in them and you help to propel them out of their victim mentality. Jesus was moved with compassion all throughout the New Testament, which caused people to be changed forever.

As I pondered all this, I was quickly reminded of my past during the times divorced moms came and visited our church. I inwardly thought about them in the same way, pitying them as if I was better than they were. In that moment I felt so ashamed. The more I thought of them, the more I began to grieve for all the single moms I had ever known. I had a new heart for them, an overwhelming compassion and understanding of how they really felt, and a love for them that only God could give.

Through all of this I came to the realization that with God's help, I could try not to self-righteously judge another person's situation ever again. Every situation is unique and only God can judge the thoughts and the intentions of others.

> "Do not judge and criticize and condemn [others unfairly with an attitude of self-righteous superiority as though assuming the office of a judge], so that you will not be judged [unfairly]."
>
> " For just as you [hypocritically] judge others [when you are sinful and unrepentant], so will you be judged; and in accordance with your standard of measure [used to pass out judgment], judgment will be measured to you." Matthew 7:1-2

Since I was in such a vulnerable state, I really needed to find people who had Jesus' compassion to help me overcome my "poor me" attitude. I loved the different churches we had been blessed to be a part of and the people were all wonderful and loving. But I just didn't feel like we fit in. I think the only reason why was because the main focus and overarching vision of these churches was ministering to the "whole" family, with a strong emphasis on the father as the leader and provider of their home and very little or no emphasis on the broken or widowed family who had no father in the home.

I knew there was a desperate need in our society to teach fathers how to lead their family. But since I was newly divorced and Troy was no longer in our home, my children and I continually felt like we didn't fit in, which made our grieving much harder to endure.

Many Sundays I wanted to just stay home and hide so that I did not have to face my new reality and the real world. My children and my parents were my only motivation to keep fighting. Their love for me and for God helped me to continually seek Him and step out my comfort zone to face and embrace my pain head on.

I began praying God would show me a church that was "ours," so we could get plugged in and continue to heal and grow together. We finally found one that seemed to have what we were looking for. I had communicated with the pastor and his wife a few times but had not yet visited the church. The greatest selling point was that the church had Royal Rangers and Girls ministries that met separately for boys and girls ages five to eighteen.

I will never forget walking up to that church building for the first time. For some reason I was extremely nervous. I think it was because this church reminded me so much of our church in Florida, or maybe it was because my parents usually went with us to church, and they weren't with me. Or most assuredly it was because I was just newly divorced.

Whatever the reason was, when I was about to open the church door, I glanced over to my right and noticed the reflection in the window of me and all of my children. Instantly, fear and shame tried to rear their ugly heads. I thought, *Look at me, an abandoned, divorced pastor's wife with so many kids. What is everyone going to think?*

I felt so awkward and insecure that I wanted to grab my kids and run back to my truck. But instead I faced my fear and boldly walked inside with a big fake smile on my face. As I looked around I felt like every single person in the church was staring at me. I decided to let Dalton and Audrynn go to kids' church, which was a huge decision since we usually all sat in church as a family. Weston, Adelynn, Azaliah, and I all sat in the back row.

Tears began to stream down my face as I glanced over at the pew to the right of me and saw a beautiful pregnant mother with her husband holding their oldest child, worshiping God together as one. My heart just ached as I longed to be the one who had that pregnant belly and my husband and kids right beside me glorifying God as a whole family.

It was also difficult battling with the lies in my head that I used to be a somebody and now I was a nobody. As I was listening to the pastor, memories of our former church flooded my thoughts.

God, it's just not fair. I prayed. *MY husband used to be the pastor, and MY kids used to be the ones everyone doted over and loved on because they were the pastor's kids. I used to be the one the women in the church usually went to if they needed advice. Now, no one even knows my name.*

Going to church with the new status of "divorced" was difficult for me. It was a sorrowful death I had to grieve. A constant pain stabbed my heart and caused me to close up and be so ashamed of my situation. Despite my insecurities, I still continued attending this church every Sunday. There were a lot of quality families and the pastor had such a heart for God. Many people became aware I was a single mom with five kids, so I didn't feel as awkward. Most importantly, I left each Sunday encouraged and strengthened to make it through the next week, which made me want to keep returning. On top of all that, my kids loved it and were thriving in every way.

On one particular Sunday morning as we were driving to church, I don't know why but I felt such a need to bring up a miscarriage I had about ten years before. Riding in the car was usually the perfect time to teach and talk to my kids about things because they were all buckled in and I had their full attention.

I told them they had a baby brother in heaven. They all couldn't believe it. I explained to them what a miscarriage was and when it happened. Up to that point Troy and I just tried to ignore it. We never named the baby or embraced him. This really bothered me, so I felt we needed to grieve as a family the life and death of their brother. I told them how old he would have been and when his birthday probably was and that they would see him again one day in heaven. We even named him Lincoln that day in the car. They were all so fascinated about it, especially Audrynn, and they asked many questions.

After church that day, Dalton, aged seven, said, "Mom, you won't believe what Audrynn said in kids' church this morning. I was so embarrassed I hid under my chair!"

He proceeded to say that the children's pastor asked if anyone had any prayer requests and Audrynn raised her hand and said, "Please pray for my mom. She just had a miscarriage. My baby brother is in heaven and she is sad. Please pray for my dad. He lives in Texas and I haven't seen him in a really long time."

I couldn't believe it. Of all the times to share about my miscarriage! We had been going to this church for a few months, so the children's pastor knew I was a divorced single mom. Therefore, after hearing Audrynn's prayer request, I was sure he probably thought I was some promiscuous single mom who had a different father for each of my children, especially the baby who was supposedly just in my stomach.

I was so upset that on our way home, I actually raised my voice at Audrynn. I explained to her in a firm way that my miscarriage happened many years ago when daddy and I were still married and that she shouldn't have asked for prayer for me. At only five years old, she of course was very sad and confused.

We laugh about it now, but after that incident I was so disappointed at my reaction, because it was another instance when I obviously still had much pride and shame about what people thought of me. It also made me see that my pride and shame was transferring to Dalton and probably to all the other kids, causing them to be ashamed of our situation as well. Later I told Audrynn I was so sorry I got upset with her and thanked her for asking for prayer for me.

Fighting shame was a daily battle. Many nights I cried and lamented that our family was not whole. I prayed many times petitioning God to please help me not be so ashamed of myself and of my situation. The hardest part about everything was the fact the kids never got to see their dad.

I tried to find children's books online and at the library that explain on a child's level what divorce is. But every book talked about how the child now lived in two different homes and gave tools on how to handle going back and forth, while living with mom one week and dad the next. I could not find one book that talked about how to handle the problem of not ever getting to see your dad. The only books like that were books about the death of a parent.

One night as I was putting the kids to bed, Adelynn asked me, "Do you think God knew when you got married that you and daddy would not be together one day? And if so, why did he let you get married in the first place?"

This was such a profound question from a nine-year-old. I said a quick prayer asking God for help and responded by telling her that I believe God did want us to get married, but that God made each one of us with a free will, meaning her daddy and I had a choice to live for God or to live for ourselves. At first when she asked me this question, I really wanted to say things that put Troy in a bad light, but I knew in the long run this would not help Adelynn heal the right way. It is crucial for them to know that there is always two sides to every story. I wanted my children to have the freedom to come to their own conclusions about their mother and father. Doing this helped me to speak to her, not out of my hurt, but with truth and clarity. Adelynn seemed to understand a lot better, but I could tell she was still having a huge battle in her mind trying to grasp everything that had already happened so far.

One night as I was reading the Bible, I looked up the word "shame" and found a beautiful passage of Scripture Isaiah 54:4-6 NASB

> "Fear not, for you will not be put to shame; and do not feel humiliated, for you will not be disgraced; But you will forget the shame of your youth, and the reproach of your widowhood you will remember no more."

"For your husband is your Maker, Whose name is the Lord of hosts; and your Redeemer is the Holy One of Israel, Who is called the God of all the earth."

"For the Lord has called you, like a wife forsaken and grieved in spirit, Even like a wife of *one's* youth when she is rejected," Says your God."

These verses encouraged and excited me on so many levels! Every time I read it, I wanted to dance around the whole neighborhood. Over the years I heard people say, "God is my husband," but after reading and rereading that Scripture, it finally became a revelation and a reality in my life. God really was my husband. We really were a whole family. My kids did have a father, a perfect father who would never leave them nor forsake them. God promised me that I did not have to be ashamed about my situation anymore, nor was I an outcast to society. Being divorced did not define who I really was.

To really understand that God was my husband and He would actually help me forget the shame of my singleness and abandonment, brought so much hope and encouragement to me. The more I grasped and believed this amazing truth, the more I embraced myself in a healthier way. Slowly, I began to accept my singleness instead of hiding from it. I started to see myself as a beautiful, whole woman, specifically created with special gifting and talents to make a difference in the world. It was so freeing to finally be confident with my children and teach them that God really was my husband. They did not have to ever be ashamed of who they were and what their family looked like.

Very rarely did I ever invest in just me and when I did, I felt guilty about it. As I became more of a whole person, I knew it was so important to "put on my oxygen mask first" so that ultimately I would be able to handle my children and life's disappointments in much more productive and healthier ways.

The pastor told me one way I would feel more connected and more a part of the church was to join a small group. As hard as it was, I stepped out of my comfort zone and over time decided to join the divorce care group and running class that our church offered. Thankfully these classes did not meet all at one time. They met during church so each of my kids had their special class to go to.

While being in the divorce care group I was given another opportunity to grow and heal. It was full of power-packed video messages and workbook pages that brought a lot more clarity, healing and resolution to me. I loved it so much that I went through it twice. Through this class I met some quality women with whom I was able to develop sweet relationships.

In the past I loved playing sports and was very active, but running was never "my thing." Even after getting many chiropractic adjustments, I was also still suffering with stiff necks every so often. I was fearful I might damage my neck further while running. So joining the running class was a bit intimidating at first. But Dan, our leader, embraced me with open arms. His leadership, the testimonies from the others, and the videos were very authentic and relatable, which left me inspired and motivated to become a better person, not only physically, but also spiritually.

I started out running five minutes and then ten and then fifteen and soon thirty minutes. Running started to actually become an outlet for me, the more I ran, the more I wanted to run. I felt so free and alive. I would listen to praise music and worship God as I ran. Without me even realizing it, God was healing my neck!

The day finally arrived when I was to run my first 5k race with my friends and many others. Running over the finish line with our blue "Run for God" shirts on, seeing all five of my kids and my faithful parents waving homemade signs, cheering me on, blessed me more than words could say.

Our running group had a private Facebook page so people could share things about their journey as a runner. I wanted to post about my healing so God would be glorified and others might be encouraged.

I would like to share a testimony of how God healed me while I was in the Run for God class last year. I had always been very active and loved playing different sports, but after having my fifth child, I was out of shape.

In 2009, I got whiplash and was suffering from severe stiff necks two or three times a week. I was very fearful about running, thinking it may jar my neck. I started applying what Don and the principles in the "Run for God" book said to do.[5]

I was amazed how the more I ran, the stronger my neck became! It has been almost a year now, and I have not had ONE stiff neck since! I would like to encourage you to do hard things and allow God to minister to you and through you as you glorify Him while you are running!

My pastor was right. As I continued attending these life groups, I did begin to step out of my pain and discomfort. Most importantly, I realized how vital community is. I saw others in a new light. God had given me special families who really loved us. They didn't just have sympathy on us, their motives were pure. They had true unconditional love and the Jesus compassion I desperately craved. God used them many times to really encourage and help us in every way they could, which tremendously helped to propel me out of my victimized state.

I really believe if I had not bravely taken the first steps to attend church and these life groups, allowing my children to get involved, too, we might not have received the deep healing we needed, nor would we have reaped the benefits of these miraculous situations. God was quickly restoring us in ways only He could orchestrate. It was so refreshing to start to see my children and me really thriving. Like it says in Joel 2:25-26, God was restoring the years the locust had eaten. We were healing, happy and we had an unspeakable hope and peace about life and our future.

"And I will compensate you for the years That the swarming locust has eaten, The creeping locust, the stripping locust, and

---

5 Run for God [Mitchell Hollis 2010]

91

the gnawing locust—My great army which I sent among you. "You will have plenty to eat and be satisfied And praise the name of the Lord your God Who has dealt wondrously with you; And My people shall never be put to shame."
Joel 2:25-26

CHAPTER 9
Planted And Not Buried

Spring time finally arrived. We were thrilled to have the snow gone and my parents' home from Florida. Just like spring, I had a fresh new life being born, and my perspective on things was much healthier. I was starting to really see our situation in a healthy way. Satan was trying to bury me, but what he didn't realize was, he buried a seed. He unknowingly planted me, He had not buried me. I was determined that with God's powerful Mercy and Grace, no matter what came my way I was going to bloom where I was planted. My Children and I were actually alive and blossoming into unique, colorful flowers of strength and beauty.

My classical tutoring job was coming to an end for that school year. I thanked God that He helped us make it through. It was such a humbling honor to get my eyes off of my own problems and focus on the eight children I had been entrusted to tutor and to help them remember everything they needed to know.

Adelynn tried out for memory master, which was a huge undertaking. There are hundreds of passages in all different subjects. This included the whole chapter of Ephesians 6, that she had to memorize throughout a twenty-four week period. When she finished she would be tested and if she achieved 100 percent accuracy, she would be labeled a "memory master." She worked really hard and got it!

I was really encouraged by her. Despite what she was going through, she was determined to be an overcomer. Dalton and Audrynn were given the Bible memory award because they sang the whole chapter of Ephesians 6 with very few errors. They were only age seven and five. That day I stood in awe of how children really could memorize many things if they had the opportunity put before them.

Azaliah was finally weaned, potty trained and sleeping through the night. She was no longer hard to handle as when she was a baby. She communicated her thoughts better, was able to sit for longer periods of time and continued to love to learn and do hard things. Her fun and curious personality radiated out of her pure blue eyes. Her passion for life was so inspiring. She was living up to her middle name, Hope, because she gave me hope so many times when I felt like quitting. She adored her memaw and pawpaw! She wholeheartedly embraced my dad as her father and shared a very special bond with him.

Weston had such a passion for politics. At ages eleven and twelve, he read books by authors such as Glen Beck, Sean Hannity, and Mark Levine. When he was little, he would tell me he wanted to be the president one day. Because of this passion I searched around and was able to find a terrific Christian ministry known for its teen-oriented programs on leadership, citizenship, and government. In this program, Weston had the privilege of visiting the Florida and Ohio State Houses and learned all about how the state legislation works. He even got to write his own bill and then present it on the real senate floor. As he got older, he actually had to prepare speeches and present them in front of his peers. I loved this. I learned so many things about our government right alongside Weston. This program built much godly confidence in him and taught him amazing speaking and leadership skills.

However, the past eighteen months had been hard on Weston. He tended to hold things in and tried to be strong for everyone. Both my parents and I noticed him express some frustration in certain situations. I also saw him start to lose his passion for politics and for reading in general. He had been closest to Troy out of all the children. Troy would take him to work with him quite often. Weston helped his dad as the grounds keeper, janitor and the sound man at our church. He really missed his dad.

So when that same Christian political group offered a chance of a lifetime, to take boys ages fourteen to eighteen out in the wilderness and help build them mentally, emotionally, physically, and spiritually, by living in the outdoors in extreme conditions, Weston begged to go.

Even though it was extremely difficult, I let Weston go. At fourteen years old, he rarely went and spent the night at other people's houses, let alone go on far away trips by himself. But I talked to many leaders who confirmed that I should let him go. In fact, the main leader lived only about half hour from us. He was a godly husband and father and was bringing two of his sons who were about the same age as Weston. He even offered to take Weston with them in his car.

After praying about it, as hard as it was to let him go, I thought this might be the perfect way for Weston to break away from the stress and to help bring healing to his hurting heart. He ended up getting a scholarship, which I thought was a huge answer to prayer. For only $20, someone sold him a huge box full of real military clothing, winter coats, rain coats and boots that were actually his size to wear.

Weston was so excited. I saw a new passion and desire for life in his eyes. They travelled all the way from Columbus, Ohio, to Fort Benning, Georgia. For one month they lived as "army rangers." He slept under the stars every night and worked really hard. He got to do many amazing things. He shot guns, ate rations and was dropped off by a helicopter to complete difficult land navigation courses. He creatively made his own harness so he could learn to repel traditionally and Aussie style. He had to build primitive shelters, learn general survival skills, first aid, and so much more. Most importantly the leaders weaved Jesus, Bible reading, and building character and integrity throughout the whole trip.

There were nights it got unseasonably cold for Georgia, down into the thirties. I worried about him and prayed for him all the time. Sometimes fear would cause me to think he was not going to survive. A couple of times, I actually called the base camp and asked how he was doing. His commander said one boy had to be admitted to the hospital. He had not taken his socks off to let his feet breath. His feet started to get gangrene. The commander reassured me that Weston was doing great.

When he came home so happy, healthy and more alive than he had been in a long time, I was so glad that I let him go. He had been surrounded by godly men and was able to learn about self-discipline and God's love right out in raw nature. He had been given a constructive place to vent his frustration and hurt. I was so proud of him, that he made it through. When he got out of the car, I gave him a big, long hug. He felt taller, stronger and older. I thought, *Wow, he left as a boy and came back a man.*

Weston was very thankful I let him go on the trip. In fact, I noticed a new inner strength in him, a strength only God could give. He was very confident of who he was in Christ. He didn't care what people thought of him. Whatever his friends wore or did, he liked to be different and start his own fashion trend. I believe this special adventure was truly God ordained. It prepared him for the decision that he made after he graduated from high school, to enlist full time into the Air Force.

Besides faithfully attending our church on Sundays and Wednesdays, we also attended a Bible study on Friday nights. This was hugely beneficial for all of us. It was another part of our healing journey.

The church had a place to go in the country, about forty-five minutes away, that bonded us together as a family and as a community. In the summer months, we would meet in a huge barn that was built in the 1800s and situated on over three hundred plus acres of farm land. This barn over looked a huge pasture of horses and sheep. These trips excited me on many levels because I have always wanted to live on a lot of acres with my own garden and animals. I thought it would be immensely cool to one day try to live off our own land. Seeing such a place in actual reality was very inspiring to me.

The kids looked forward to this little get away every week. They would bring their Bibles and listened intently to the study and then loved to answer all the questions. Azaliah sometimes had a hard time sitting still, but learning about God in such an intimate setting was very encouraging.

Adelynn was my little Bible scholar. Even at only nine and ten years old, she would answer questions in the most profound way. Many times the parents asked me how she knew the Bible so well. All I could say was, "God is giving her an insatiable desire to know Him more." The man who led the Bible study was a pastor and after many months of attending, he offered to baptize anyone who felt like they were ready.

"We want to get baptized, Mom," said Adelynn with Weston right beside her. I told them they could, but when I did, I had a twinge of disappointment. I thought, *I want Troy to be the one who baptizes them.* It would have been such a beautiful memory and bonding time to watch your own husband and pastor baptize your children as they made the biggest and best decision of their life. This was yet another pain I had to grieve and ask God to give me the grace to overcome.

After coming to terms with the fact that Troy would not be the one baptizing them, I had a peace about letting them do it. I wanted to make sure the kids understood why they were getting baptized. I printed off a little study for them and we went through it together. But I still felt they were not grasping or understanding the full reason why they should get baptized.

Baptism day arrived, and as we were driving, my dad in such a profound but simple way explained to the kids all about baptism. He told them, "Baptism is just like what happens to a cucumber when it is dipped in vinegar and comes out a pickle. You can never turn it back to a cucumber, because the vinegar changes it." He continued, "Baptism is a beautiful representation of the forever change that happens when you make the commitment to allow the vinegar (Jesus) to change you into a pickle (a new creation)."

He told them to remember their baptism day forever, because it would always remind them of the day they asked Jesus to be Lord of their life. He encouraged them by telling them that all their sins and bad things they had ever done had all been forgiven and that they were now a new and changed person.

"Therefore if anyone is in Christ [that is, grafted in, joined to Him by faith in Him as Savior], he is a new creature [reborn and renewed by the Holy Spirit]; the old things [the previous moral and spiritual condition] have passed away. Behold, new things have come [because spiritual awakening brings a new life]." 2 Corinthians 5:17

I was relieved that Weston and Adelynn completely understood everything my dad was telling them. That day, I had a greater appreciation and admiration for my dad than I could even put it into words. I was immensely thankful for him, for his leadership and all the sacrifices he was making to help my children, his grandchildren, become all God had called them to be.

Weston and Adelynn courageously went into that April's ice cold river water knowing exactly why they were doing it! I was so thankful Dad was videoing it because when they came up out of the water, they had the biggest smiles on their cold little faces.

As I wrote in my journal that night, after watching my children get baptized, I was overwhelmed with thankfulness and praise to God because of how He really was restoring and healing us in unexpected, profound ways. The more I saw that God was going to provide and that my children really were thriving in the midst of not having their father in their lives, the more I thought that with God's help, I might possibly be able to survive living out on my own.

The past two and a half years of living with my parents had been very hard, but at the same time, it was one of the most meaningful and special times of my life. I thanked God for every good time and every bad time, because we were now better people. Eight people were forced to make a living, eating, going to the bathroom and sleeping all in very tight quarters work. Yes there were tears; yes there was yelling; yes there was sickness, bad attitudes, fears, and failures. But I would never trade the unforgettable memories we made, the special tight bond my children got to make with their grandparents and the huge sacrifice my parents made so we could heal and get back on our feet. We did life together and we made it through.

My parents were my heroes, my best friends and my confidants. The adoration and appreciation I have for them cannot be explained in words. Our love for each other ran deep. I felt so honored that my children and I got to spend so much quality time with them.

Thinking more about the possibility of living on my own and being my children's sole provider was intimidating and a little frightening. Despite my inhibitions, my search for housing began. Having five children made things a lot more complicated. I looked at hundreds of different apartments and rental homes. I couldn't believe the outrageous prices: $1,200 to $3,000 a month was ridiculous and unaffordable for me. All the rental agencies I talked to said I had to have a three to four bedroom home because of the ages and sex of my kids. I looked into Section 8 housing. There was a seven year waiting list unless I was homeless and living on the streets. Finally after many weeks of searching and a lot of prayer, I came across Habitat for Humanity.

This seemed like the perfect opportunity. I looked at all the qualifications and decided to make a call to our county first. I found out they built in really dangerous neighborhoods. I called other counties and one wasn't too far from my parents' home and my church. I decided to set up an interview.

They were extremely nice and helpful. They came to my parents' home to fill out a questionnaire and make an assessment of my family and me and what our living area looked like. They recorded my credit score and how much I was making with my tutoring and receptionist jobs. After their evaluation and many days of waiting, I finally got a letter congratulating me on being qualified to build my very own Habitat for Humanity home. I could not believe it. I thought my credit might be too bad because one of our houses in Florida had been foreclosed on and my name was on it with Troy. Thankfully, the seven years was almost over, and it didn't adversely impact my credit.

They told me my house payment for a four bedroom home would only be about $400 a month with a loan that was interest free! I was so excited I could barely breathe. Having a home to call my own was a dream that didn't even seem possible. They said it usually took about two years to finally get into a house. I would need to put in a total of two hundred and fifty hours working on other Habitat homes as well as my own. I would need to complete one hundred hours before I could pick out a lot.

I did not waste any time. I passionately and quickly finished my one hundred hours. It was truly a memorable experience. I worked with many volunteers who were mostly in their sixties and seventies and I enjoyed every minute of it.

I learned how to nail things, put shingles on, put in the base floors, caulk, paint, sand, measure and so much more. If I brought lunch, I would get more hours for that day. Most of the time I brought homemade egg salad, sloppy joes or turkey sandwiches and they would be so thankful for everything that I brought. I thoroughly enjoyed our conversations and loved their servant hearts and their passion to work hard. Watching them selflessly sacrifice their time to volunteer was a huge inspiration to me.

On November 15, 2011, I finished my one hundred hours for Habitat for Humanity. I couldn't have done it without my mom, dad, Weston, and Adelynn's help. They watched the younger kids and temporarily took on a lot of my responsibilities. It was such a satisfying but humbling experience to accomplish something completely out of my comfort zone. During that time Jesus infused me with a strength I never dreamed I had. I could see such relief in my parent's eyes knowing I would eventually have a place to call my own.

"I can do all things [which He has called me to do] through Him who strengthens and empowers me [to fulfill His purpose—I am self-sufficient in Christ's sufficiency; I am ready for anything and equal to anything through Him who infuses me with inner strength and confident peace.]"
Philippians 4:13

Habitat said if everything went as planned, I could be in my home by November 2013. This meant we would only need to live with my parents for two more years. This was such tremendous news. I was scheduled to pick out a lot within the next few months. I now had a goal, a reward and something to motivate me while we continued living with my parents.

CHAPTER 10
Our Gentle Giant

"Call 911!" Weston yelled as he ran through the front door. "Grandpa fell in the garage and is hurt really bad." I immediately called for the ambulance while my mom and I both ran out in the garage to check on my dad. I knew it was bad when I saw him lying unconscious on his back with blood draining from both ears.

The operator told me to try to turn Dad on his side in case he would vomit and choke on it. I got on top of him to try to turn him but I couldn't budge him. He started to get sick so I turned his head to the side. That's when I noticed a huge puddle of blood under his head.

I laid my head on his chest screaming and crying, "Dad, Dad I need you, please don't leave me!" He immediately sat up for a brief minute and we locked eyes. His beautiful brown eyes said more than words ever could, "I am so proud of you and I love you very much!"

"No Dad, No! Don't give up, keep fighting!" I cried and prayed, *God, please heal him. Help him. Don't let him die!*

I happened to glance over at my mom. She was in shock. All she could do was stare and pray. I prayed so hard, so fervently and so desperately. The ambulance finally arrived after what seemed like an eternity. I could tell my dad was trying to fight because even though he was unconscious, the EMT kept saying, "Stop moving, Mr. Foster." My mom followed my dad in the ambulance to one of the top hospitals in Ohio and they had a team of surgeons waiting.

After they left, I ran to check on my kids. Without me knowing, Weston had grabbed all of his siblings and immediately took them to the back bedroom so they wouldn't hear anything that was going on. My children at the time were ages fourteen, eleven, eight, six, and three. Adelynn had told me later, they all were crying and wondering if Grandpa was okay, but Weston was praying and reassuring them. Knowing Weston did this for his siblings, encouraged and empowered me in so many ways. He is definitely, a hero in my eyes.

I called my pastor so he could pray with me and so we could put Dad on the prayer list. I contemplated whether or not to go outside to the garage. I wanted to try to figure out what happened but was fearful about it. I decided to go look. Dad must have climbed up in the attic, tripped on a wire and fell through the ceiling. He landed on a tricycle that rolled and caused him to fly backwards and land on the back of his head.

As I stared at all the blood on the garage floor and the big hole in the attic ceiling, a deep sorrow embraced me. I started crying uncontrollably. Flashbacks of our last conversation flooded my thoughts, replaying in my mind over and over. I blamed myself, thinking, *If I just hadn't mentioned the boxes in the attic, then he wouldn't have felt like he had to go up there.*

It was a beautiful, abnormally warm and sunny Saturday, November 26, 2011. It was the day before my parents forty-eighth wedding anniversary. They had just returned from a wonderful trip to Cape Cod with my brother and his family. My kids were overly excited to have them back home, especially the little girls, Audrynn and Azaliah. Their normal ritual every morning was to run into my parents' bedroom and jump on their bed to say good morning and pray with them. My dad loved to daily say the Lord's Prayer. My mom let them play with the bed remote for a little bit, allowing them to move the bed up and down.

Mom was so excited to show the girls all the shells they found on the beach in Cape Cod, and my dad, Weston, and Dalton were extremely excited about the football game they planned to watch that afternoon. It was so cute how Dalton wanted to dress just like his grandpa and how after he saw his grandpa, he ran to put on his matching Ohio State sweatshirt.

Before they went to Cape Cod, my parents had put their house on the market because they wanted to find a house with a different floor plan. Surprisingly it sold faster than they ever thought it would. While they were gone to celebrate their forty-eighth wedding anniversary, the inspectors called and said they were coming to look in the attic to check for mold. They told me there was no need to move anything out of the attic because they had special tools to work around things. That fateful morning when I was on my way home from my favorite food pantry, I remembered that I forgot to tell my dad about the inspectors. I called and told him they were coming to check the attic Monday morning, but he did not need to go up to move any boxes.

He told me okay and then he asked if we could all watch the Ohio State verses Michigan game together as a family. I told him yes, but regretfully wasn't too thrilled about it.

When I got home from picking up bread, I remember passing Dad on the sidewalk. He looked so festive in his trendy white Ohio State sweater with red trim and white Ohio State baseball cap that really highlighted his olive complexion.

I told Weston to put all the bread in the freezer in the garage that I got from the "free store," and that is when Weston found Dad. It all happened in a fifteen minute time frame.

After sending out e-mails and getting a prayer chain going, I couldn't believe the outpouring of love and support from so many people. It was overwhelming how they came out of the woodwork. People from my church, Bible studies, homeschooling groups and family all offered to watch the kids, cook meals or do whatever we needed them to do.

About this time I went to go check on the kids and told them Grandpa had fallen out of the attic and hit his head. He was now at the hospital having surgery. I gave them all a long hug. The fear and sadness in their eyes broke my heart. I hated leaving them, knowing how devastated they were, but I knew I had to get to the hospital. I called one of my friends and asked her to watch my children while I went to the hospital. I called my brother, David, on the way to the hospital. I was crying so hard, I could barely talk. David and my dad were really close. The amazing thing was, David was still driving home to Illinois from Ohio, after he and my parents had gone to Cape Cod together. He happened to only be at the Ohio and Indiana border. Immediately, he turned his car around and was with us within two hours.

I then called one of my close friends, Kristin because, ironically, she worked in the brain and trauma unit at the hospital where they took my dad. Kristen was another friend that was an amazing source of encouragement to me. Her love for God and for people was such an inspiration. Our friendship was God ordained. She was able to call the nurses and relay back to me what was going on. She told me that the best brain surgeon was working on Dad and they were ready to operate as soon as my dad came through the hospital door. It was such a comfort and a relief to know that Dad was in the best possible care. He ended up surrounded by Christian nurses. One nurse stayed by his bed and prayed all night for him. Later I found out that the paramedic who worked on my dad in the ambulance, was not only a Christian, but actually went to our church.

After the surgery, the surgeon came out and said the operation was successful, but he also said that there was extensive brain injury and the only thing we could do was wait and Pray.

When I saw Dad for the first time with all those tubes in him and his head swollen, I just couldn't stand it. I went to him and held his hand, but he gave no response at all. Right then I knew deep down he was already gone, but all the while I still hoped and believed God could do a miracle.

Despairingly, within twenty-four hours the doctor told us that Dad's brain was completely dead and only the machines were keeping him alive. My dad had never wanted to be kept alive by machines, so with much prayer and conversations with family, we chose to shut off the machines. Dad was completely gone within a few minutes on November 27, 2011, my parents' forty-eighth wedding anniversary.

God, why? I prayed. *My mom is now left as a widow and my children and I are left without a father and grandfather. We miss him terribly. We are heartbroken. My dad was the only father Azaliah really knew and the only stable father figure in my kids' lives. He took care of us. He loved us unconditionally. We need him!*

I just couldn't seem to stop crying. My pastor and his wife and the youth pastor and his wife came to pray with me, but I was deeply mourning and couldn't seem to get a grip. Knowing Dad is now in heaven was the greatest comfort for me. He longed to go to heaven. To think he was pain free and without any stress or problems to worry about was profusely reassuring to me.

On November 27, 2011, I sent the following message to everyone we knew:

It is with a heavy heart and very downcast spirit that I let you know my dad died today! It doesn't seem fair; it doesn't make sense; but it happened. We lost a patriarch of the faith, a father, grandfather, provider, rescuer, encourager, prayer warrior, and a teacher to my children. He loved his wife with his whole heart! They had been married for forty-eight years today! I know God has a purpose in this, but right now I do not see what that purpose is. Please continue to pray for my mom, my children, my sister, my brother and their children. We love you all!

The hospital took a print of my dad's hand right after he passed away and gave it to us. Below his hand print was a beautiful poem about death. I came home and gathered all my kids into the living room and showed them the handprint and read the poem to them. I tried so hard not to cry as I told them their grandpa was no longer with us and was now living in heaven with Jesus. They all began sobbing. Azaliah didn't really understand, but the rest were devastated. I just saw Weston's eyes lose hope. He had been praying so hard that God would heal his grandfather.

Adelynn wanted to know more details. I told her the doctor said Grandpa's brain was dead and the machines were keeping him alive. So, following Grandpa's wishes, we unplugged life support. Adelynn got very mad, she cried and screamed and said, "Mommy, why did you take him off life support? God could have healed him."

It took the kids a while to truly come to terms with the reality that their Grandpa was gone. For many months after he died, Azaliah would tell everyone she met that her grandpa fell out of the attic and got a boo boo on his head and was in heaven.

While planning the funeral, my mom and I went to visit her pastor. He answered some deep questions and gave us more clarity on why this might have happened. We left his office knowing that God was still in control. We might not see it yet, but He had a purpose for our pain.

The funeral was overwhelming to me. The love and support from hundreds of people was outrageous. It was an open casket. At first when I saw my dad in the very sweater he died in, it was very difficult for me. His face was a bit swollen and he did not look like my dad.

My dad was such a handsome man with a beautiful olive complexion, dark brown eyes and a dimple in his cheek and his chin. Seeing him not look like himself was hard. I also had to make the difficult decision of whether or not to let my children see their grandpa in the casket. I knew it would be good for Weston and Adelynn, but Dalton and Audrynn were only eight and six. I decided to leave Azaliah with a babysitter and let the older ones see their grandpa, because I read that it really helps a child grieve and it brings finality to the situation.

Not only did they bravely see their grandpa in the casket, Adelynn, Dalton, and Audrynn courageously sang all of Psalm 91 in front of everyone. Watching them sing as they stood in front of their grandfather's open casket is a picture I will never forget. They sang every verse all the way through with such passion, love, and honor. As they sang, the presence of God filled that little funeral home in the sweetest, most profound way. There was not a dry eye in the place.

We were all privileged to say something meaningful about my dad at the funeral. My mom exuded beauty and grace as she talked about her husband of forty-eight years with such love and adoration. As I got up to share, I looked at the hundreds of people staring back at me, but this time I didn't care. I wanted them to know what a special person my dad was. Below isn't exactly what I said but it sums it up the best way I can remember:

I would like to honor my dad and share with you a few of the things he taught me. He left a legacy, and his influence on my life resonates within the walls of my home. My dad was a gentle giant, and when he spoke, people listened. This taught me not to talk unless I have something to say.

My favorite Christmas present was when I was nine years old. Dad picked it out and wrapped it all by himself, a beautiful pink sweater with a kitten knitted on it. This taught me to be a thoughtful giver!

Dad took us camping every summer with a ministry called "Camping with Christ," which taught me how to serve others in ministry.

He provided for my wants and my needs. He taught me security.

He sent me to Christian school my whole life and went to most of my basketball, volleyball, and softball games to cheer me on. He taught me to believe in myself.

I wrote a poem when I was eighteen. He loved it so much he hung it in his office and sent it to every ministry he could think of, hoping it would touch someone's life. This taught me that I have giftings and callings that are worth sharing.

At the age of twenty, when I started seriously dating, Dad shared with me Ecclesiastes 7:1,

"A good name is better than precious perfume, and the day of one's death better than the day of one's birth."

He told me to guard my name, my character and integrity, more than anything, for that is the only way people will truly see Jesus in me.

My dad rarely showed physical affection, but I will never forget when I was going through the most difficult time of my life. I was about to get on an airplane and he kissed me on the cheek and said, "Erica, I love you!" This taught me unconditional love.

He loved his wife, my mother, until death, forty-eight years, which taught me faithfulness.

He loved my children dearly and told me, "Erica, God has given you five smooth stones to raise. They are the righteous seed. Don't ever lose sight of that."

He selflessly helped provide for me and my five children for two straight years while we lived in his home.

The greatest, most valuable lesson he taught me was through watching him continually turn to his heavenly Father for guidance and wisdom even in the midst of his failures and imperfections. This taught me that no earthly father should ever take the place of my heavenly Father.

In the pouring rain, I watched my dad being buried in the same graveyard we used to visit together when I was a little girl to put flowers on our ancestors tombstones. The pain was extremely unbearable. However, knowing my dad was in heaven was a comfort beyond any human explanation. I had an unwavering assurance and excitement that he wasn't in that casket. He was healed and alive and I would undoubtedly see him again one day. As it says in Revelation 21:4: "and He will wipe away every tear from their eyes; and there will no longer be death; there will no longer be sorrow and anguish, or crying, or pain; for the former order of things has passed away."

The house was now sold. My mom closed on it only a few days after the funeral. Because the house sold so quickly and my dad died so suddenly , my parents never had a chance to find another place for all of us to live. Gratefully, my dad made sure the selling contract stated that we could rent for six months from the buyer if we needed to, until we found a place to live.

A Tribute to my beloved husband, Daryl D. Foster
May 21, 1942 – November 27, 2011
They say opposites attract. That was definitely the case with us. Daryl was easy going and contemplative. I was high energy and made quick decisions. Daryl was serious, I was lighthearted. Daryl had a dry sense of humor, and I liked to laugh out loud. Daryl was a deep thinker; I responded more from the surface level. Daryl was more formal and followed protocol, whereas I was more down to earth. Daryl was more timid and reserved. I liked to be the life of the party! Daryl was more of a home body and I wanted to socialize. Daryl was kind and gentle and I was more outspoken and to the point..

We had our first date on September 13, 1963 and married two months later on November 27. We both accepted Jesus as our Savior within one year of each other and God turned our lives upside down for Him. Instead of us being at odds with each another, God taught us how to become One. It took most of our married life to become one, but we did it. God blessed us with three children (one son and two daughters) and 12 beautiful grandchildren. Only God could have made a way for us to have our honey moon and last week together at Cape Cod celebrating our 48th wedding anniversary, along with our last dance!

Daryl was the most handsome and humble man I ever met. When we were with friends, and even family, Daryl usually didn't say a lot unless it was important. Our daughter-in-law, Angelia, once described Daryl as "A quiet leader whose authentic nature made people feel at ease and one who could lead many and never realize it." God gave him a good business mind and wisdom. He was extremely loyal – to God, to me, to his children, his grandchildren, his job and church.

Daryl was also very generous. There were many times I stood in awe over his extreme generosity to others.

We served the Lord together for almost 40 years. I give God the glory for holding us together. We often prayed together and we saw God move over and over again because of our prayers. I always knew Daryl loved me. From the time we met he treated me with respect and affection. He told me often how much I blessed his life. He loved and respected his parents. He promised his dad that he would remember them every year on Memorial Day by putting flowers on their graves, and we never missed one year.

Daryl adored our children. He would have done anything for them. He rescued each one of them at various times in their lives while growing up and as young adults. I loved Daryl's dry sense of humor. Sometimes I would wake up in the middle of the night and burst out laughing because of something funny he said or did (probably because I finally "got it").

Daryl would never think that he made a difference in someone else's life. When I would complement him he would brush it off and not feel deserving of it. Daryl left me, his children and grandchildren the greatest legacy any man could leave his family. And that legacy is his relationship with God. He loved and followed Jesus with all of his heart. He laid down his life for all of us.

Our granddaughter, Sophie, left the graveside service in turmoil because of the loss of her grandpa, but on the way home she fell into a sound sleep and had the following dream which she shared with me; "Grandpa was in the back yard at the Cape Cod place and everything was alive except a pink rose. Grandpa was watching over the garden and taking care of it by pouring out love, money and affection. He looked really tired. Then he looked up and saw the rose and tiredly picked it up with a glowing smile and began rising up to heaven while looking at me. God had his arm around him and calmly said to me, He's fulfilled his purpose on earth and is now with Me."Sophie was then at peace.

The reason I am doing as well as I am is because of God's faithfulness and Daryl's commitment to follow God's plan. God took him on our 48th wedding anniversary to show me two things; one that

He held us to our vows to the very day and, two that He is in charge of our lives! I honor my husband and thank God that when Daryl passed on to be with Jesus, I was able to have a priceless satisfaction in my heart that we had resolved all issues with one another and could both say, "No regrets" and have only the pleasure of our memories to recall.

Erica had a dream after Daryl passed on. And here is what she saw: "It was exhilarating and so real. I was in this beautiful, freshly painted red barn and a supernatural peace surrounded me. The sunshine was magnificent and the warmth of the rays was so comforting. Out of the blue, my dad triumphantly walked in with the glory of God surrounding him. He had a head full of thick, black hair. He looked at me with such love and compassion and his smile at me was intoxicating and breathtaking. His teeth sparkled and were as white as snow as he was saying, "I have boldness now, Erica!"

Jesus allowed me to see Daryl in heaven - clicking his heels in the air and rejoicing. He is now free and happy forever! I miss him every day and yet I know that he wouldn't want to come back. I'm looking forward to heaven more than ever before. It will be the most glorious day!

These scriptures represent Daryl's integrity and character:

Micah 6:8 He has shown you, O man, what is good; and what does the Lord require of you, but to do justly, and to love kindness and mercy, and to humble yourself and walk humbly with your God?

Proverbs 11:3 The integrity of the upright shall guide them.

James 1:12 Blessed, happy, to be envied is the man who is patient under trial and stands up under temptation, for when he has stood the test and been approved he will receive the victor's crown of life which God has promised to those who love Him.

Loving wife Carol

Getting back to reality after the funeral was heart wrenching. Everywhere I looked in the house there were memories of my dad, which caused me to continually cry. I actually started back to work right away at my nursing home job just to try to get my mind off my pain.

I came home from work one night a few days after the funeral and found my mom sitting in her favorite, hunter-green rocking chair, trying to rock Azaliah to sleep. I asked her how her day went and the more I conversed with her, the deeper the compassion and concern I had for her. Sorrow and grief emanated from the very depths of her soul, shooting out of her beautiful green eyes in the most desperate way. She had already suffered a few panic attacks and some other minor health issues before my dad died and now she no longer had a husband to comfort her nor a home to call her own.

She told me in the most loving and gracious way that she didn't know if she could physically, spiritually and emotionally handle the pressure of having six people all living under her roof. I didn't blame her. She needed some time to heal, grieve and get clarity without so much stress continually bombarding her. She would never kick us out of her home. She would die before she would put us out on the street, but she just didn't know what to do.

In that moment, the realization of how serious our situation was hit me head on. The last thing I ever wanted to do was to bury both of my parents, especially within such a short time from each other. I ran out to my truck, locked myself in, and started screaming and crying at the top of my lungs, all the while banging on my steering wheel.

God, WHY? This is too much for me to handle. I am husbandless, fatherless, and now a homeless mother of five children! I don't know what I am going to do!

I knew I wasn't really "on the street" homeless, but at that moment I felt like I had nobody to turn to, nowhere to go and nowhere to live.

I remember driving around my neighborhood in such agony I could barely breathe. A taunting relentless fear and hopelessness gripped me stronger than anything I had ever felt before. It was the first time in my life when I felt I needed something tangible, a drug, alcohol to get drunk, a man to embrace and have sex with me, whatever and whomever to numb me. I didn't care anymore. I just wanted the pain to go away.

I felt stuck in the valley of the shadow of death—the death of my dream of being married for life, the death of my dad and the only godly male role model that we all had. There was the death of having the comfort and security of a home to live in. All this added to the fearful thought of being forced to take care of five young kids completely on my own was more than I could bear. At that moment, the luring temptation to run away from God was fiercely strong.

Do you hate me, God? I screamed. *I have faithfully served You my whole life, and this is my reward?*

As I was crying out to God to save me, imploring Him to take away the unbearable pain, I heard an almost audible voice say, "Go see Pastor Dave." It couldn't have been any clearer. So with much hesitation and fear, I went to my pastor's house. We had only been going to his church for about six months, but he had helped with my dad's funeral and was very familiar with my situation.

It was dark out and no lights were on in his house, but I bravely knocked on the door anyway. To my surprise, Pastor Kay, his wife answered. She could tell I had been really crying hard and asked me to come inside. Pastor was on the couch and asked me what was wrong. I told him how distraught I was about my life.

I told him my mom had just sold the house and it would be two more years until my Habitat for Humanity home would be built. I told him my mom would never kick me out, I just knew that if we stayed with her any longer , she might die from the stress.

I cried in desperation, *I just don't know what I'm going to do. I can't afford any other housing and I have five little people that I need to provide for. I am utterly distraught and have so much pain that I can't even think straight!*

After I poured my heart out to Pastor Dave and his wife for quite a while, he calmly said, "So basically you need a place to live." It was the first time I cracked a smile and said, "Well, that would solve a lot of my problems." He got up out of his chair and asked his wife to go into another room with him. Then he came back to get me and said he had something he wanted to show me. They took me downstairs. There was this huge and vacant living area. Pastor Dave and his wife said, "You can live here if you want." I started sobbing uncontrollably and gave Pastor Kay a huge hug. I couldn't believe that God would provide so quickly. Pastor said that a family had just moved out a month prior. As they took me from room to room, I saw a glorious unfolding of God's amazing grace. There were three bedrooms and two full baths. The girls' and the boys' bedrooms were surprisingly painted the same colors as Adelynn's and Weston's bedrooms that had been Florida. They were violet and hunter green. There was a little kitchen with a stove and refrigerator that came out into a quaint family room that already had furniture in it. It had an outside entrance so we wouldn't have to go through their house every time we went somewhere. Right across the street, there was a beautiful park the kids could play at.

I left my mom hopeless and distraught but came back home to her hopeful and encouraged. When I told her all God had done, she was extremely relieved, thankful to Pastor Dave and amazed over God's mighty and quick provision in our lives.

Within in a week's time, Pastor Dave, Weston, Dalton and I all worked together to move our stuff into the pastor's basement. It all happened so fast. We got each bedroom set up, and we were able to get settled in just in time for Christmas.

PART III
THE DANCE

"Life isn't about waiting for the storm to pass
It's learning to DANCE in the Rain."

Vivian Greene

CHAPTER 11
Comfort In The Cave

Have you ever found yourself in a cave? Not a real physical cave, but a cave of despair and despondency where the darkness seems to just swallow you up and everything seems to be closing in around you? Do you know that God does some of his best work in those cave experiences?

I called the pastor's basement "the cave," not because it felt like a cave, but because I felt a lot like David did in the Bible when he felt rejected and stripped of everything on his way to the cave of Adullam. David felt abandoned by God. However, while in his cave, God showed David amazing truths and brought unbelievable healing and restoration to his life.

> David therefore departed from there and escaped to the cave of Adullam (1 Sam 22:1).

It had only been one month since my dad passed away and I was still deeply grieving. It was Christmas time and morosely, I did not have any desire and little money to get presents for my children. Thankfully, a big local business and my church adopted my children for Christmas. After putting all the kids to bed thinking they might not wake up to any presents, Pastor Dave came down with the many presents given to us. He also gave me a little Christmas tree that I tried my best to decorate.

The next morning the kids woke up to a decorated tree and a room full of presents including six bikes. It was a moment that will be etched in our minds forever. To see each one of my children shockingly surprised and overwhelmed by the goodness of God was the greatest Christmas present I could've ever received. Their radiant smiles and unending laughter brought healing to my broken heart. As they were opening their presents, the presence of God was undeniably strong in our little family room and I had a strong desire to read Isaiah 54:4–17 out loud to the kids.

After I was finished reading, I was crying and pleading with my children, "Look around you. You have a roof over your head, food in the refrigerator, a warm bed to sleep in, and presents surrounding you. Please don't ever forget this moment and always know that my Maker is my Husband, and God is and will always be your daddy. You have nothing to be afraid or ashamed of because He will always provide for us!"

Christmas was on a Sunday that year and we decided to attend the morning service. The pastor asked if anyone wanted to share anything. I felt a little tug at my dress and Audrynn, age seven, kept saying over and over, "Tell them, Mommy. Tell them!"

I finally bent down to her. "Tell them what?" I asked.

"Tell them that God is my daddy!"

Tears immediately flooded my eyes because in that moment I knew she got it. She truly understood that no matter if her earthly daddy and grandpa were gone; she has a Daddy who would never hurt her, never leave her and always provide for her. That morning as I looked down the pew at each one of my children praising God with such a peace surrounding them, I saw a beautiful confirmation and reminder that God really is who He says He is and He will do what He says He will do.

Only a few weeks after Christmas, Troy called us and told us his dad had died of a massive heart attack. This really hit me and the older kids hard. The younger girls didn't get to see this grandfather as much. We really loved Grandpa Mac. His humor and love for his wife and for life was such an encouragement to us all. We had many special memories of the special times we spent with him. It was yet another sorrow to have to heal from.

The more I realized I was surrounded by a community of believers who wouldn't let me fall, the more of God's comfort I received. Many people came to my rescue. The support was truly overwhelming. I felt like I was being held, supported and strengthened by a bond that was stronger than anything I could ever imagine. I felt humbled and thankful to be a partaker of their help.

> "And though one can overpower him who is alone, two can resist him. A cord of three strands is not quickly broken." Ecclesiastes 4:12

> "Carry one another's burdens and in this way you will fulfill the requirements of the law of Christ [that is, the law of Christian love]." Galatians 6:2

> "For where two or three are gathered in My name [meeting together as My followers], I am there among them." Matthew 18:20

My friends put us on a meal schedule for a couple of weeks, and people brought us delicious homemade dinners so I wouldn't have to cook. I couldn't believe the many cards, gift cards, cash, checks, gifts and babysitting that people gave us, but most importantly the constant prayers and encouragement.

One of my favorite gifts was a beautiful afghan the church gave me that had Psalm 23 woven on it with a beautiful picture of a lamb and his shepherd in the valley.

> *The Lord is my shepherd,*
> *I shall not want.*
> *He makes me lie down in green pastures;*
> *He leads me beside quiet waters.*

He restores my soul;
He guides me in the paths of righteousness
For His name's sake.
Even though I walk through the valley of the shadow of death,
I fear no evil, for You are with me;
Your rod and Your staff, they comfort me.
You prepare a table before me in the presence of my enemies;
You have anointed my head with oil;
My cup overflows.
Surely goodness and loving-kindness will follow me all the days of my life,
And I will dwell in the house of the Lord forever. (NASB)

I read Psalm 23 over and over because it gave me such comfort and hope, since I truly felt stuck in the valley of death. My heart was overwhelmed with gratitude for every person who selflessly gave to us. I continually prayed that God would bless them for blessing us.

As the weeks and months progressed, I still continued to daily battle deep sorrow and grief. Even though I was extremely thankful to God for providing us a temporary home, living in a whole new environment without my parents or my husband was at times excruciating and lonely. I longed for a man just to hug me, encourage me and validate me. I missed my dad very much. I am sure the pastors heard me on the many nights I cried myself to sleep.

Only with God's amazing grace and help did I choose to keep turning to Jesus Christ and feel and embrace my pain instead of giving in and trying to find someone or something to numb my pain.

Through my desperation, I began seeking God and asking Him to show me what I could do so I wouldn't feel such heartache and sorrow. One of the greatest things I began to do was to sing praises to Him. I have always loved to sing. I remember many times being in the shower as a teenager and my brother would bang on his bedroom wall yelling at me to stop singing. For some reason this time was different. Maybe it was because

I was so desperate. I don't know, but the more I sang, the more of God's presence filled our little home. I sang constantly, in the shower, cooking, cleaning, doing dishes, driving in my car, and even grocery shopping. I would make up songs singing; I would memorize Scripture singing; I would say prayers singing; I would put the girls to bed singing all of Psalm 91. We would sing about the names of God and other encouraging praises to God. I would sometimes drive my kids nuts while singing. Even the pastor told his congregation he could hear me singing through the vents (quite embarrassing).

Many times I didn't even know I was singing or why I was singing. I did know one thing, the more I sang to Jesus and proclaimed His awesomeness, the more of an overcomer I became.

As I started studying the benefits of singing, I began to realize what a powerful tool singing praises and worshiping God really is. God's Word actually tells us to sing to Him always.

> "Do not get drunk with wine, for that is wickedness (corruption, stupidity), but be filled with the [Holy] Spirit and constantly guided by Him.

> "Speak to one another in psalms and hymns and spiritual songs, [offering praise by] singing and making melody with your heart to the Lord;"

> "Always giving thanks to God the Father for all things, in the name of our Lord Jesus Christ." Ephesians 5:18–20

> "I will bless the Lord at all times; His praise shall continually be in my mouth." Psalm 34:1

I also had the astounding realization that when David was in his cave, he continually sang praises to God as well. Singing ignited my faith to believe the impossible was possible. When I didn't believe the words I was singing, the more I sang them, the more I believed the words. Singing praises brought the presence of God into my home, which gave me a supernatural joy and an unexplainable peace in the deepest part of my being. I no longer felt empty and alone. In His presence, I was able to endure my trials so much better. There were times when I literally felt God's presence in our midst. This was so baffling to me because chaos, fear, sadness, and suffering could be surrounding me, but I had an inner knowing that everything was going to be all right.

"In Your presence is fullness of Joy." Ps. 16:11

Sickness could not live when I worshiped God. The kids were rarely sick, but Azaliah every now and then would have wheezing episodes and get croup. Each time I had to reluctantly give her breathing treatments. One night she was coughing a lot, had a high fever, and I had enough of it. I rocked her and sang Scriptures over her all night long until her fever broke. This was another time I could actually feel God's presence surrounding us. I knew God healed her that night, and from then on she no longer needed breathing treatments.

The more I sang or listened to music that glorified God, the more the atmosphere in our home would be relaxing and refreshing. Even my kids felt the peace.

Another awesome thing that singing praises to God did for me was help me to obey God. Singing made war on my temptations. Praise quiets the avenger. Just like when police officers tell criminals to raise their arms in surrender, as I would raise my arms in praise to my Creator and surrender all my junk to Him, the more empowered I was to look temptation square in its face and tell it to leave me alone.

"Through the praise of children and infants you have established a stronghold against your enemies, to silence the foe and the avenger." Psalm 8:2

Singing got my mind off of my own problems and put my eyes on the magnificent, majestic, perfect character of God. It caused me to be so thankful and so honored to know Him. Nothing else seemed to matter anymore. But most importantly, God was glorified when I sang to Him.

Even on a practical level, researchers say that something positive happens to our brain when we sing. I have read that scientists have actually studied the elated feelings associated with singing and have discovered we release endorphins, the "feel good" hormones, when we sing. This explains the emotional response so many of us have when we hear our favorite genre or song. Other studies say that the hormone released when we sing is oxytocin, which generates feelings of intimacy and connection. This could be why studies have found that singing reduces feelings of depression and loneliness.

I didn't always have a desire to sing. Many times I would be in such agony that it was just too hard. There would be days I would fall to the ground crying and begging God to take my pain away. But, when I sacrificially chose to praise God was when His comfort would be the strongest. The times that I praised God even when I didn't feel like it, were the times I believe, I blessed God so much that He wanted to be with me even more. Just like when my children do something for me that I know took a lot of courage and sacrifice, it makes me want to bless them, give to them, and be with them so much more.

"Through Him, therefore, let us at all times offer up to God a sacrifice of praise, which is the fruit of lips that thankfully acknowledge and confess and glorify His name"
(Heb. 13:15).

Through singing, I began to truly understand from experience the unexplainable comfort of the Holy Spirit.

"And I will ask the Father, and He will give you another Helper (Comforter, Advocate, Intercessor—Counselor, Strengthener, Standby), to be with you forever— the Spirit of Truth, whom the world cannot receive [and take to its heart] because it does not see Him or know Him, but you know Him because He (the Holy Spirit) remains with you continually and will be in you." John 14:16–18

"I will not leave you as orphans [comfortless, bereaved, and helpless]; I will come [back] to you." John 14:18

As the Holy Spirit comforted me in astounding ways, I realized I was actually blessed to have sorrow. Not the hopeless sorrow of the world that is full of despair, but a godly sorrow that is full of hope, joy, and freedom. This sorrow caused me to be so desperate for God that I wanted nothing more than to be in His presence.

"Blessed [forgiven, refreshed by God's grace] are those who mourn [over their sins and repent], for they will be comforted [when the burden of sin is lifted]" (Matt. 5:4).

"Paul adds, "For [godly] sorrow that is in accord with the will of God produces a repentance without regret, leading to salvation; but worldly sorrow [the hopeless sorrow of those who do not believe] produces death" (2 Cor. 7:10).

Another thing that God showed me to do, was to serve others more. This was hard, because I barely had the time to serve my family, let alone others. I was tired and still hurting. But all throughout the Gospels our greatest leader, Jesus, is described as a servant. Jesus humbly washing the feet of his disciples is a beautiful representation of pure servant hood. I knew that if I would start thinking about others instead of myself, my pain would be easier to bear. Over the years I loved to serve others. In Bible College I had learned practical ways of how to serve in ministry. I worked in children's church. I volunteered helping special needs children. I helped with the homeless ministry, the prison ministry and volunteered quite often in the church nursery. I would counsel women one on one whenever there was a need. However, over the years of raising children, dealing with my failing marriage and many heartbreaks, I slowly started getting disillusioned about church and ministry all together. This ultimately, caused me to loose my desire to serve in the church. I loved to serve my immediate family on a daily basis but it was now time for me to step out of my pain and start helping others again. Thus began my new journey of serving and volunteering at our church.

This activity was huge and extremely instrumental in my healing process. It was a big stretch for me, but the more I served others in our church and community, the more I got my eyes off of myself and my problems. Most of the time I would try to serve with some of my children with me, by doing this I could still be spending time with them, since my time was very limited. I tried to go to our church prayer meeting almost every Tuesday morning before work at 6:00 a.m.focusing most of my prayers on others and not myself. At first I had to force myself to do it. Then I eventually looked forward to going. I volunteered in the nursery and in the preschool once a month with Adelynn. We all tried to help the pastor as much as we could by babysitting his grandkids, serving during outreaches, or doing anything else he asked us to do.

After a year of healing and embracing my pain, I really started having a heart for other single moms. I did some research and found a great video-led curriculum by the same makers of the "Divorce care" class I had already taken. With Pastor's permission, I started a six week class on single parenting. This was extremely difficult for me, but it propelled me out of my comfort zone and in the process brought an amazing healing and clarity to many.

Each of my children and I were excited to serve in the church's yearly Easter and Christmas plays. My children were sometimes given a singing or a speaking part, which really helped them to get their eyes off of their own situation. They felt so honored to be able to help the pastor win people to Jesus and follow Him:

"For even the Son of Man did not come to be served, but to serve, and to give His life a ransom for many" (Mark 10:45).

Being a good steward of our things, our money, and my body was another area where I believe God wanted me to grow. I did not want to be a burden to my pastor, nor did I want to take him and his wife for granted, so I offered to pay a monthly rent.

I made sure I paid my tithes to my church and I continually strived to always stay out of debt.

I believe God was teaching me to live a simple life. Losing many of my material possessions, even precious and irreplaceable things like baby albums, journals I wrote in since I was a senior in high school, and photo albums caused me to have a massive appreciation for the things that really matter most. "People are more important than things," was one of my favorite sayings.

No matter what we are doing, I daily try to have an eternal perspective on things and ask myself quite often:

"Are the things you are living for worth Christ dying for?"
Leonard Ravenhill[6]

I was also determined to be a good steward of my mind and body by keeping it pure. After my dad passed away, my mom honored me with a beautiful ring my dad had given her on their thirtieth wedding anniversary. I cherish this ring. I put it on my left ring finger and made a vow to God that I would not have sex with a man until I had the privilege of getting remarried. I had only been with one man, my former husband, and with God's grace helping me, I was determined to keep it that way. I also wanted to pursue mental purity as well. I knew the more I thought, studied or filled my mind up about sex the more desire I would have for it. There were times when I was tempted to read magazines on sex, watch movies, or read books that had love stories with sexual scenes in them. I chose not to. My dad's ring was my purity ring, a tangible reminder to always stay pure.

It wasn't always easy living in a basement. The walls and ceilings were very thin, the windows were very small and the people upstairs probably could hear everything that was going on. This made us sometimes a little on edge. As much as we tried, we had days where we fell apart. Pastor came down a few times in the midst of an intense argument or fighting either between the kids or between me and the kids, to see if there was anything he

---

6 Leonard Ravenhill, [www.leonard-ravenhill.com/quotes]

could do. I remember one time in particular. He came down in the midst of Weston and me getting upset with each other. He immediately defused the situation and brought us all in the living room where we held hands in a circle and just prayed. After we were finished praying, the peace was restored back into our home. This brought more unity and a greater perspective on things.

Sometimes I would still have pity parties. Turning forty while living in the cave was not fun. I felt old, ugly and wrinkled. I was in complete denial of it. Most of my friends who were forty had husbands to enjoy life with. My special friend Deena greatly encouraged me when she surprised me with a 40th birthday party and specially wrapped forty gifts just for me to open. With each gift I unwrapped, I felt so honored and loved.

My healing didn't come all at once. I had to make daily choices of whether I wanted to succumb to my own desires and feelings and follow my own footsteps which were the easier route, or choose to do the harder thing of turning to God and follow His footsteps. The astonishing thing was the more I chose to obey God, the more I wanted to obey Him. And the more I wanted to obey Him, the freer I became.

Establish my steps and direct them by [means of] your word; let not any iniquity have dominion over me. Psalms 119:133

I love what Benjamin Franklin said, "Only virtuous people are capable of freedom." This is profoundly true. When I choose to do things in my own strength and disobey God, I start to feel the chains of fear, hopelessness and bitterness choking me all over again. It is definitely hard work to face my pain and follow God's way, but having His presence with me at all times is my greatest motivation. When I'm daily in His presence I no longer feel anymore pain or despair. **It is the best drug in the world!**

CHAPTER 12
Beauty from Ashes

"Erica, would you consider being my executive secretary?" One Sunday morning at church an amazing dear couple - named Craig and Heather came up to me, and Craig asked if I would like to be his secretary. I stood before them in shock. "Me? I don't have any experience in that field at all, nor do I have a degree or even a resume."

Craig said, "Anyone who can raise five kids on their own must have some skills." He continued telling me that as long as I had integrity and a willingness to learn new things, I would do great.

This couple was a beautiful representation of Jesus in my life. They poured out their time, resources, and encouragement on us continually. In the midst of raising and homeschooling her many children, Heather continually believed in me, loved on me, and valued me as a friend. She would selflessly cook meals for us, buy us special gifts and always remember each one of my kids' birthdays. Her prayers for me and constant encouragement to keep homeschooling were relentless. And best of all, my children and her children hit it off and got along great!

Craig asking me to be his secretary was such an honor. He told me he knew I still wanted to homeschool, so I could come in at 7:00 a.m. and leave at noon. And he would pay me almost double what I was making at the nursing home job. I took his offer very seriously. I prayed about it and talked to Pastor Dave and my mom about it. I most definitely and excitedly decided to take the job.

This job changed my life in many ways. Craig was the vice president and corporate controller of the finance department of a huge health care system with over 20,000 employees. For many years, this business was voted as one of the top one hundred companies to work for in the United States. Walking in the first day and seeing my name and title posted on my own desk, next to my own window looking out at hundreds of skyscrapers, thirty-three floors up, was an experience I will never forget. I was surrounded by top executives and had no time to wallow in my fear and intimidation.

I had to learn Word, PowerPoint, Excel, Microsoft Office, and so much more. I was in direct communication with the secretaries of the CEO and CFO. Craig had about ten directors under him. I remember the first time I had to schedule a meeting for all the directors. As I reserved the room, sent out invitations to each director's calendar, and put together the PowerPoint slides for Craig to present, I was astounded how God gave me the grace and the clarity to do it all. When he asked me to be in the meeting with him, I couldn't believe it. It was so surreal. I was so humbled and in awe as I thought Craig must really believe I have value if he wanted me to accompany him to this meeting.

As I fearfully sat in that big conference room with ten executives surrounding me, I literally was flabbergasted. I thought, *I can't believe God helped me put this whole meeting together and it is actually running smoothly.*

Craig believed in me and saw greatness in me even when I didn't see it myself. He didn't even think twice about it. He just said, "Erica, I need you to do this." My continual internal question would be, *Me? I can't do that.* But I had to find a way to make it happen. I had to look fear in its face and conquer it head on.

At times I made mistakes. I was so mentally stretched, but Craig and God continually believed in me and motivated me to learn hard things. This gave me the confidence to continue striving harder.

A few weeks after I started working for Craig, I was having a rough day. God encouraged me through a life-changing event that I wrote about in my journal and shared with some of my friends, in hope that it would encourage them.

October 2012

I don't know about you but I have days when it's very difficult to truly grasp who I really am in Christ. Today was one of those days. As I was driving home from work, God brought me back to something that happened when I first started my job as an executive secretary.

My boss, Craig, told me that one of his direct reports had done something ethically wrong over the course of six months and it had adversely affected one of the branches of the company's finance department. He told me that I needed to take care of this immediately, not by e-mail, or by phone, but to just go find the vice president of human resources and bring her to him.

At that moment I was thinking, Me? Can I really do that all by myself? So with some fear and trepidation, I went and found her, interrupted her meeting, and told her that Craig needed to see her right away! She said, "Okay, let's go!"

I was shocked! I couldn't believe that just like that I was able to just go get the vice president of human resources in a company with over 20,000 employees. While I was in the elevator taking her up to my boss, there were two other vice presidents with us. One said to the vice president of human resources, "You have Erica escorting you. This must really be important." When he said that, I thought to myself, I am nothing but Craig's secretary.

It was at that moment I realized that since I was escorting the human resources director in the name and the authority of my boss, I was able to accomplish much in Craig's realm of authority. God used that situation to show me what can happen in the spiritual realm when we truly take on the authority and power of His name.

In the natural, I am just a struggling, single mother of five children. But when I take on the NAME of God, I no longer am husbandless. My maker is my husband! (Is. 54!)

I am no longer fatherless, Abba Father is my Daddy!

I am no longer poor. Jehovah Jireh *is my provider. "I have not seen the righteous (those in right standing with God) abandoned, or his descendants pleading for bread" (Ps. 37:25).*

My mind is no longer in turmoil because Jehovah Shalom *is my peace that passes all human understanding!*

I am no longer overwhelmed because Jehovah Nissi *is my banner of victory. I am an over-comer by the blood of the Lamb and by the word of my testimony!*

I am no longer lost because Jehovah Rahi *is my Shepherd! He leads and guides me. Never will He leave or forsake me.*

I am no longer full of sin because Jehovah M'kaddesh *is my Holiness and* Jehovah Tsidkenu *is my righteousness. I am made pure through His Word and I am in right standing with God!*

I am no longer sick, for Jehovah Rapha *is my healer. By His stripes I am healed!* [7]

The list goes on and on...

Wow! This has truly revolutionized my thinking! I have been trying to do so many things in my own strength! Today I am trading my name for God's name, so I will no longer live in defeat or discouragement anymore!

This revelation of how powerful we are when we take on the names of God was such an encouragement to me. It gave me more boldness and clarity in everything that I did. The hours I worked at my corporate job, 7:00 a.m. to 12:00 p.m., ended up being great. I did sadly have to resign my classical tutoring job and my nursing home job, which made homeschooling a lot more difficult. Since we moved farther away from Weston's

---

7 [What are the different names of God and what do they mean? www.gotquestions.org/names-of-God.html source of names for God.]

Christian school, he now attended the local public school. It was a difficult decision, but he ended up fitting in great. Many times I seriously thought about putting all the kids in public school. It was getting harder to homeschool with my new job. In fact, I felt like a failure many times. I even put them in part time school classes at times hoping it would take some of the pressure off.

Despite all the frustrations, we persevered and kept schooling at home. I let the kids stay up late reading, doing school work, or playing quietly in their rooms. This meant they would sleep in the next morning. I would go to work and they would stay asleep until around 10:00 a.m. Adelynn would make breakfast and they would all try to do their chores together. Usually by the time they were finished I was nearly home. After I got home I would relax for a little bit and then we would have school together.

The more I sought Jesus to comfort us and heal us, the more His presence would be with us. Sometimes He would even comfort us in tangible ways. The times I wanted to give up the most were the times He would send someone or something to encourage me right at the perfect time. About once a week a card would come in the mail addressed to me and be signed by Jesus. These cards comforted me in the most unexplainable ways. I really think the person who sent these cards prayed over them first, because when I read them, It felt like Jesus was actually speaking to me. They continued coming for many months.

One time I came home from work to find a whole dozen roses. The card said, "All my love, Jesus." This was very encouraging to me because my dad's favorite flower was the rose. I stood in amazement that anyone knew. It really felt like my dad sent me those roses to reassure me how much he and Jesus really loved me.

I was shocked when out of the blue a big local church called and said they were doing a contest for their Women's conference and someone had submitted my story to be considered as a possible candidate for their "Woman of the Year" contest. She told me that there were hundreds of entries but only 8 would be finalists. She said that each contestant would get a free makeover, and a brand new outfit to walk on stage, while they shared their story in front of the whole audience. She said the winner would win over $1,000 in gift cards to different restaurants and stores. She then excitedly told me that my story was chosen as one of the eight. Tears of gratitude welled up in my eyes as she continued talking. I was very humbled and could not believe that I was one of the ones chosen.

After nervously walking on stage in front of hundreds of women modeling my new outfit and hairdo, while they told the audience my story, I was shockingly called out as the winner. I began crying, as the pastor's wife handed me a huge bouquet of flowers and gave me a big hug. Me? Woman of the Year?

As I stood on the stage looking out into the big audience, I was in awe and overwhelmed by the goodness and mercy of God. There were many days I felt very ugly, insignificant and inadequate but this situation brought another tangible knowing that God was for me and not against me. The guest speaker was the amazing Dani Johnson. God spoke through her to me in profound ways. She had a similar story as mine. She has five children and was homeschooling them. At one point She was homeless, divorced with no money but God turned her tragedy into triumph and she stood that day as a beautiful, successful entrepreneur, making millions of dollars. I left that conference with a new found hope and an insatiable desire, that I too could possibly one day become and entrepreneur, so that I would have more freedom to be home with my children.

Pastors Dave and Kay were huge blessings in our lives and a continual support when we needed them the most. We enjoyed being with them and their extended family so much. Their grandchildren would come down to the basement often to play with my kids, which caused them to create a great bond with one another. Pastor Kay always remembered each of our birthdays and blessed us with a special gift.

Every time the basement door opened and Pastor Dave yelled down, "Do you guys have plans for dinner?" We would drop everything we were doing and run up the stairs. Eating around a table with a whole family and seeing pastor interact with his wife, children, and grandchildren brought healing to us in ways that I can't even put into words.

Pastor Dave loved on my kids as if they were his own grandchildren. He took the girls to the yearly daddy daughter date nights He taught the boys here and there by letting them help with yard work, putting on car brakes and going to widow's homes to fix a problem, and so much more.

I believe the main reason that God brought pastor into our lives was to help bring healing to my kids' broken hearts. They desperately needed to see and feel a tangible father's love. Who could be better than a pastor? He reads to the kids every Wednesday night after church. This blesses me beyond measure and is definitely an unexpected answer to prayer. Over the years he probably has read fifty books or more to them. These books were not just ordinary books, they were handpicked with the goal of teaching my kids godly character, which would in turn ignite in them a deeper passion and desire to become more like Jesus.

The pastor's dog, Sanders, adored us. Every time the upstairs door to the basement opened, Sanders ran down to be with us. He was an adorable, long haired, red dachshund. He would roll on his back and wave his paws in the air wanting us to pet him every time we saw him. It got to the point where he continually scratched on the door and cried to come down and see us.

One Wednesday night after Pastor was finished reading to the kids, he excitedly said, "I was just given a German Shepherd puppy and I want you to have Sanders." Immediately the kids all started jumping and screaming and giving the pastor a lot of hugs. They were so excited to finally have a special dog to call their own, especially a dog like Sanders. Sanders brought so much healing to the kids. He would sleep on each child's bed and lick them and love on them continually. Dalton loved to rub the hair on his ears and Adelynn loved to have him to sleep right on her pillow.

My kids absolute favorite thing to do was attend family camp. I would save up money from my tax return so we could go each year. They would probably choose to go to family camp over anything. This camp was called the Great Family Adventure. It was put on by the Assemblies of God. It runs over the Fourth of July week and is where a whole community of believers come together to camp in tents, eat from the fire, swim, hike, go to classes and worship God. Families from our own church would all camp together in one area. We would all help with cooking meals and cleaning dishes. Since the camp had hundreds of acres of fenced property, I felt at peace letting the older kids just freely ride their bikes all over with their special friends. This yearly camp brought an astounding healing and unity to my kids and me.

During this time, God was also doing amazing things with my mom. She was able to find a darling patio home for herself. It was something she always wanted. God's comfort and peace was all over her. She had a great support system and special friends who ministered to her and encouraged her all the time. The more I thought about our situation, the more thankful to God I was for how things worked out. My family living with Pastor Dave and Kay and Mom living on her own were answers to prayer. My mom was able to continue being a grandma to my kids but also have alone time to heal. She came quite often to get one or two of the kids at a time and spent quality time with them. We were always there for each other if she or I needed prayer and a listening ear. She walked as a widow with grace, dignity and a bold knowing that her Maker was her Husband.

We were very disappointed that Troy rarely called and only came two times to visit during the two years we lived with the pastor. Looking back now, I believe his absence was another huge blessing in disguise and actually God ordained. At the time, Troy was still walking in anger and blame towards me, and to be bombarded with that negativity would have thwarted our healing in so many ways.

"As for you, you meant evil against me, but God meant it for good in order to bring about this present outcome, that many people would be kept alive [as they are this day]."
Genesis 50:20

While living in our "cave." I was astounded to see that the God was definitely turning our mourning into joy and our ashes into beauty. As it says in Isaiah 61:3:

"To grant to those who mourn in Zion the following:
To give them a turban instead of dust [on their heads, a sign of mourning], The oil of joy instead of mourning, The garment [expressive] of praise instead of a disheartened spirit. So they will be called the trees of righteousness [strong and magnificent, distinguished for integrity, justice, and right standing with God], The planting of the Lord, that He may be glorified."

CHAPTER 13
Home Is Where The Heart Is

The kids really didn't want to move, they felt so comfortable and safe living in the pastor's basement. We were in walking distance from our church and the kids had their close friends living within five minutes from us. Pastor even told me we could stay at his home for however long we needed too. I knew as much as we loved it, we couldn't live there forever. Now that we were more healed and whole, I felt confident to continue with my plans of building our Habitat for Humanity home. I had already picked out a lot to build on and they just needed me to sign the agreement. This was another huge and a bit frightening decision because once I signed the contract; I couldn't get out of it for many years. But again I prayed about it, and talked with my pastor, my mom and many other close friends before I decided to go ahead and sign the contract.

I finally got the other one hundred and fifty hours in that I owed, working on my home and other Habitat homes. It was hard work putting in all the hours and going to all the mandatory classes teaching me how to take care of a new home. Thankfully, Weston at age fifteen was able to help in the Re-store, adding to my hours. Even though, it was exhausting and draining, at the same time it was so rewarding and life-changing. To see a community come together to help families in need was such an inspiration. I learned so much not only about how to build my own house but also how to reach out of my suffering to help other families in need to build their houses too.

My mom and I prayed that Habitat would build my house with a basement. It would be such a relief to have somewhere to store things and to run to in case of emergencies. So I went to the director asking him if he would consider adding one. Of all the many houses they have built over the years, they had never built a house with a basement. Since my family was the only one so far who had so many children, the Habitat board ended up deciding that I really needed to have one. We all were beyond excited and so thankful for this added provision in our life.

The basement was poured, and it was time to start building the walls. I had never seen it done this way, but a whole church came together and built them right on their church property. They had different areas where volunteers were trained to do different things.

My mom, my kids, and I actually got to help nail many of the 2 x 4s together. It was beautiful thing to watch a whole community of believers come together to help us. Everyone wrote Scriptures, encouraging words, and pictures all over the boards of our walls. I was so impressed by the outpouring of love that I wrote the congregation so I could thank them.

Dear Liberty Church,

My children and I would like to thank you from the bottom of our hearts for how you sacrificed your precious time and energy to help build the walls of our new home! When I pulled up to the church and saw all the men, women, and children united as one just to build my walls, I was immediately overwhelmed by the love of God, and tears started streaming down my face.

We have had to endure much pain and heartache, but now we truly understand the beatitude „Blessed are they that mourn, for they will be comforted." As I cried out to God, His amazing comfort blessed us in life-changing ways. Not only did His presence comfort us, but God in His rich mercy has used YOU, the church, to minister to us in ways that only He could orchestrate.

So again, thank you for BEING the church. You have helped us to have a home of our own, and for that we will be forever grateful! We pray God's richest blessing on you and your families.

Our Habitat home was built. The striving had finally ceased. As I stared at the beautiful two story home with a basement that had our name on it, surrounded by majestic trees, I was overwhelmed by the goodness of God. To know that from now on my children and I will forever have a roof over our head was worth it all. I was beyond thankful that my church and homeschooling family gave me a house warming party and my singles group put in an alarm system, so we could move in with most of our needs being met.

Every time a family moves in to a Habitat for Humanity home they have a home dedication service for them. Many people came from far and wide to pray over my children, me and our new home. Pastor Dave shared a beautiful message from his heart of how important a home was, and I was honored they asked me to share too.

As they were praying for us, I briefly glanced up to see my five children surrounded by people who loved and supported us, was a comfort that was indescribable. God truly is a rewarder for those who follow after Him.

> As Jesus said, "But first and most importantly seek (aim at, strive after) His kingdom and His righteousness [His way of doing and being right—the attitude and character of God], and all these things will be given to you also"(Matt. 6:33).

Moving in was a bitter sweet time. We were going to sorely miss Pastor Dave and Kay. In fact, it was a little frightening to think this would be the first time in my whole life that I would be living completely on my own without a man in the house.

CHAPTER 14
Alone Yet Not Alone

A few weeks after we moved in, we had a tornado warning in the middle of the night. At first I panicked. My heart was racing and fear engulfed me as I frantically got each child out of bed and rushed them down to the basement. As I was intensely hugging my kids, I was overwhelmed with the goodness of God in our lives. I began thanking and praising Him for all the things He had provided for us. In that moment, the presence of God surrounded us in such a sweet, powerful and loving way that all fear completely left us!

It wasn't always easy living on our own. To think that all the bills were in my name and I was now the sole provider for five children was quite daunting. Even though it wasn't true, I felt like everyone left me. I didn't feel the community surrounding us as strong as they use to and we were now so far away from everything and everyone that loneliness hit me quite often. And to top it all off the kids were sad too. They missed the pastor and their friends. There were times when I had to deal with jealousy over other single moms who had former husbands that played an active role in their child's life and paid enough child support for them and did not have to worry about their child's well-being. I also dealt with the jealousy of married moms who had husbands who provided for them and had the honor to stay at home so they could minister to their husband and children. My Reality hit me hard. Sadly, there were times I lost my desire to sing.

We had to deal with some things that were quite difficult. While we were on our first vacation back to Florida since we left, Sanders ran away from the house he was staying at and we never found him. This was a crushing blow to us all. All the way home from Florida each one of us had tears of grief flowing down our cheeks. We see now that God brought him into our life when we needed him the most and we believe that a wonderful family found him and is taking great care of him.

Another difficult time was when out of the blue, my mom met a wonderful godly man through the recommendation of her dentist who was a Christian. It had been over two years since my dad died and she was very secure in her role as a widow and never really thought about getting married again. But astonishingly, they hit it off and were married within five months from the time they first met! Even though I was absolutely thrilled for her and loved her new husband, this was a bit devastating to us all. My mom was my best friend and we spent much time together and her new husband was now the center of her life, and rightfully so. The hardest part was seeing her with another man other than my dad. Pictures of my dad were being replaced with pictures of him and my mom talked about him all the time, instead of my dad. The kids and I really missed the old times. However, the more we spent time with them together as a couple, the more we embraced our new family. Jim loves us and wants to pour into our lives on a continual basis. He is the complete opposite of my dad. I think if he was like my dad it would be even harder to deal with. I am now so thankful that God brought this special man into or lives. His zest for life and his passionate love for my mom is inspiring.

After a while, I really started having a desire to get married again. I had been single for five and a half years. During that time I was mainly focused on my kids healing, my healing and even a possible reconciliation with Troy. I had men ask me out, but I knew it wasn't Gods timing yet. Now that I was living on my own , I had more of a desire for a husband . I really believed my children were healed and ready to have a father in their life. To have a godly man to do life with, to raise children with, to flirt with, to tease with, to date with, to dance with, to be best friends with , to impress and to be impressed with , to laugh with, to kiss every chance we could and to pray with was a powerful dream I really wanted to come true.

Now that I had this desire, I thought I would try getting on a few Christian dating sites. This was extremely difficult. I felt like I was selling myself. To put pictures up and tell men the great reasons why they should meet me felt so invasive, prideful, and unnecessary. I had many people tell me not to do it. I had many other people tell me it was great and they knew of people who met their best friend and lover on a dating site and highly recommended it

My older kids hated the idea, especially Dalton who was twelve. One night he asked me if he could talk to me, and he said, "Mom, it's not appropriate, and it is dangerous for you to find a man online. You need to just trust God to bring you a husband."

Despite my children and my inhibitions, I decided to go for it anyway. The process was very overwhelming and time consuming because I had many men message me and want to meet me. I felt like I needed my own personal secretary just to weed through the different profiles.

Going on my first date was hard for all of us. I was so nervous I could hardly breathe. This man treated me very respectfully. But it was so awkward and the more I talked to him, the more I saw things in him I didn't want in a husband. For about six months I continued dating and talking to different men.

I told these men up front that I was saving myself for marriage and I was not interested in a physical relationship. This stance sure did get rid of the men who had ulterior motives. I did meet a few in whom I saw potential. We would text, Skype, talk and go out together. I felt bonded to one man in particular and I could tell I was getting emotionally attached. He would say just the right things causing me to get so excited. His text messages were what I looked forward to in the morning and when I went to bed at night. I thought he really valued me.

But after meeting up with him and getting prayer and advice from my family and pastors, I knew I could no longer pursue a relationship with him. I felt terrible for allowing myself to get attached to him. What frightened me the most was when I realized I was tempted sexually by someone who wasn't yet my husband. I thanked God for that fear, because it was a healthy, wholesome fear of displeasing Him, which in turn gave me the courage and the superhuman strength to say no.

This experience gave me a wake-up call and acutely reminded me of my purity ring and the vows I made to God to stay emotionally and physically pure. After that, I knew it was time to get off all dating sites. It was affecting my kids and my emotions. There was so much tension, strife, and division in our home during that time and my poor decisions were the reason for it all!

I have kept a favorite, powerful quote by Susanna Wesley in my Bible since I was in Bible college, and read it often. God reminded me of that quote during this time of pursuing a husband and it convicted me on every level. It made me realize that I had sinned and disobeyed God.

"Whatever weakens your reason, impairs the tenderness of your conscience, obscures your sense of God, takes away your desire for spiritual things, whatever increases the authority of the body over the mind, that thing is sin to you, however innocent it may seem in itself." [8]

I ashamedly went to my children and humbly asked them to forgive me for being so selfish, and I asked God to forgive me as well.

After I got off the dating sites, I really began seeking God to teach me how to accept His love for me. I realized, I must still

---

8 Susanna Wesley [The prayers of Susanna Wesley]

have a void or an emptiness in my heart since I craved a man so badly. Through all my years of being a Christian, I knew God loved me. I was raised in church and I read Scriptures on His love many times. I even had amazing encounters with God's love. He had proven to me time and time again that He is my Husband and Father. But it seemed like over the years, I still had a tendency to doubt and not accept or receive His love on a daily basis. To really live knowing that someone so great loves me unconditionally, faults and all, seemed inconceivable.

From then on I started really studying God's love for me. I began looking up many Scriptures about God's love and started memorizing them, posting them on my mirror, and making songs up for them so I could sing them and study them. I wanted them to be so a part of my life that they would start to resonate with me anytime I felt lonely or unloved. One of my favorites is Ephesians 3:15–19:

> "May He grant you out of the riches of His glory, to be strengthened and spiritually energized with power through His Spirit in your inner self, [indwelling your innermost being and personality], so that Christ may dwell in your hearts through your faith.
>
> And may you, having been [deeply] rooted and [securely] grounded in love, be fully capable of comprehending with all the saints (God's people) the width and length and height and depth of His love [fully experiencing that amazing, endless love];
>
> and [that you may come] to know [practically, through personal experience] the love of Christ which far surpasses [mere] knowledge [without experience], that you may be filled up [throughout your being] to all the fullness of God [so that you may have the richest experience of God's presence in your lives, completely filled and flooded with God Himself]."

Wow! To think my ultimate Father is continually giving me *power* in my innermost being so Jesus can dwell in my heart is amazing! This is the reason I can fully experience God's endless, amazing, unexplainable love that He has for me, and it is all through His son Jesus Christ. Jesus loves me so much that He died for me. Even if I was the only person left on the earth, He would have died just for me. But what is even greater, His love for me is so strong that He could no longer stay in the grave. He arose three days later longing to have a personal, daily relationship with me.

To know this kind of love is pursuing me and backing me up, gives me greater confidence in every area of my life. I can't help but to sing and dance. The greatest thing is, the more and more I accept God's love, the less and less desire I have for a man. To realize that nothing I ever did or could ever do will separate me from the love of God is the most astounding reassurance. I began to embrace and enjoy my singleness in such a greater capacity that I even said to God,

"I don't have to have an earthly man to love me in order to survive. If I never get married again, I will be satisfied with just You."

The more and more I studied His Love, the more I realized what an honor and blessing it is to be "single." This was such a profound revelation to me that I posted what God was showing me on Facebook only so I could possibly help others who might be struggling with the same thing.

What is singleness?

I really am not a big fan of posting personal things on Facebook. However, if my post draws someone else closer to Christ, then it is worth it for me to be transparent and vulnerable. "By no choice of mine, I am a single mom of five children. I longed to be married for life and to pass that legacy down to my children, as my parents and grandparents did for me. But I can't." Wow! What a relief it is to say that.

For years I was so ashamed of it. I never would mention it or talk about it except to the most intimate people in my life. The people who did see me with my kids would think I was amazing or stupid .

I had to be one or the other just for having five kids, let alone raising them completely on my own. As the years progressed and I started really embracing my role as single mom, God started showing me that my true identity was not in my title but who I am in Christ and that He loved me unconditionally with such a fierce, relentless love.

As this became a revelation to me, it was still hard at times to truly grasp the fact that being single did not make me less of a person. The world's and sometimes even the church's definition has confused the word "singleness" to meaning "being alone," and therefore it left me feeling ashamed and withdrawn.

So I began to study the Bible and different books and realized that the word "single" really does not mean "being alone." I have talked with many people, married or not married, and all of them at one time or another have felt very alone.

As I began to look up some of the definitions of singleness, I discovered that the word basically means to be separate, unique, and whole. It was then I realized God wants us all to be "single" whether we are married or not. If we could truly become the unique, whole person He has called each one of us to be, I believe there wouldn't be any more divorces or marriage problems, ever!

How freeing and refreshing it would be if we as married people got our needs met first from God. What a huge burden would be lifted from our spouses who seem to always be trying to fix our problems. And what an awesome joy it would be to have two married, godly, sexy, whole, unique, not needy companions on the same team, walking along beside each other, celebrating each other's uniqueness, all the while fulfilling the call of God in each other's lives. Wow! I think there would be revival in America.

As an unmarried person, how freeing it would be to not need a husband or wife, but to be so whole and one with Christ that we can choose whether or not we want to get married. Yet while we were unmarried, we would still be the unique, unashamed, special person He so longs for us to be!

If I ever do get married again, my decision will be based on true love and companionship rather than on fear or desperation. This is my goal and I would like to encourage you all as well, married or not, to embrace and enjoy your "singleness" so you can truly become the unique, whole, special person God has called you to be.

Through all of this, I had to ask myself, *What if I would have embraced my uniqueness and my singleness when I was married and had not relied on Troy so much to meet my deepest needs? Things might have ended up totally different, who knows?* I do know one thing; I can't dwell in the past. I have to just learn from it and move on.

During this time of truly desiring Jesus' love for me, I came home after I had a rough day at work. The house was a disaster, there was a mountain of dishes in the sink that were supposed to have been washed and the kids were fighting. I ran upstairs to my bedroom, locked the door and just started crying uncontrollably. The main reason I was upset was because after working three years as an executive secretary, my job went from being part time to full time. My boss Craig got a new boss that was adamant about things and he told Craig that no executive should have a part time secretary. Craig's boss gave me a choice that day, to start working full time or to leave. It was so harsh. Craig felt terrible about it but there was nothing he could do. His hands were tied.

At that moment while sitting on my bed, I felt so alone. There I was, confronted with one of the hardest decisions ever. I had five children to provide for. I desperately needed a tangible hug. I wanted to actually *feel* God's love for me. I was so desperate that I literally started hugging my Bible. It may sound weird, but in that moment, I honestly felt Jesus' arms hugging me back! All His words in the Bible were comforting me, reassuring me, strengthening and loving me in every way. He was actually confirming what I had been studying all along about His love. With tears streaming down my face, I began reflecting and remembering my journey from the time I was a little girl until then, and right there in my bedroom, I was completely overwhelmed with God's amazing love for me. To realize that He loves me with such a pure, unconditional, relentless love made me feel so undeserving and so wretched. Why would Jesus choose to love me so much? He believes in me and He is my biggest cheerleader and encourager. He really is my daddy, my boyfriend, my husband, my everything. He only wants what is best for my children and me. Just like it says in Romans 8: 37-39:

> "Yet in all these things we are more than conquerors and gain an overwhelming victory through Him who loved us [so much that He died for us]."

> "For I am convinced [and continue to be convinced—beyond any doubt] that neither death, nor life, nor angels, nor principalities, nor things present and threatening, nor things to come, nor powers, nor height, nor depth, nor any other created thing, will be able to separate us from the [unlimited] love of God, which is in Christ Jesus our Lord."

To realize that Jesus loved me so much and nothing could ever separate me from His love was so encouraging, that I left my bedroom that day feeling like I could conquer the world.

I was very tempted to take the full time position. In fact, if I didn't have my security and foundation in Jesus and His powerful love, I know I would have. What person in their right mind wouldn't? I had my own parking spot, my own desk. I worked in downtown corporate America. I made more money than I ever had in my life. I was starting to really thrive and to top it all off, I had a wonderful Christian boss. I began to really pray and seek God on what I should do. He reminded me in such a sweet but powerful way the moment I first became a single mom. He brought me back to the time when I was at a crossroads and had to choose to either take the easy route of what the world thinks all single moms should do, or take the hard route and solely trust God for my children's provision.

The words, *Being a Mother is the highest career in the nation and God is my employer* and *As long as I put God first and train and disciple my kids to know God than He will always provide for us,* just kept playing over and over in my head.

The next day, I was driving home from the grocery store, feeling discouraged over this huge decision I had to make. I happened to be in the middle of a big city. I was sitting at a stop sign when out of the corner of my eye I saw a deer and fawn just standing in a meadow looking majestic and free. They didn't have a care in the world. There was chaos surrounding them; cars, buildings, people and loud noises. Yet they didn't budge. The mother deer remained so confident and secure in who she was and her fawn followed right alongside her. That Mother deer spoke volumes to me. In that moment I was reminded of the verse in Habakkuk 3:19:

"The Lord God is my strength [my source of courage, my invincible army]; He has made my feet [steady and sure] like hinds' feet and makes me walk [forward with spiritual confidence] on my high places [of challenge and responsibility]."

I always loved that scripture but I couldn't remember what "hind's feet" were, so I decided to look it up. A hind is a mother deer that lives in the mountains. The hind is one of the most sure footed animals in the world. When she would be running, she would place her back feet at precisely the exact location of where her front feet landed. The young deer also followed his mother step by step, placing his feet exactly where the mother hind had placed her feet. This exact tracking meant life to both the hind and her young.

God used His creation to paint a picture in my head that I will never forget. God is making my feet like hind's feet, teaching my feet to step in the exact location of where He stepped. This allows me to courageously walk forward with a bold confidence. He makes me sure footed and secure, so that I will not go off the path, even when there is chaos distracting me or temptation luring me in. What a powerful reminder that just like the young deer who followed their mother, my children were following my footsteps right behind me.

In that moment, I had to ask myself a very serious question. How would I ever be able to be that mother hind for my kids if I was gone from seven in the morning until six at night, Monday - Friday? I would come home exhausted with nothing left to give. If I only had one or two kids I might have done it. But to have five kids to take care of in the midst of working ten or eleven hour days, (if I included commute time), was not something I was physically, emotionally or spiritually equipped to do. Life wasn't about me, my job and money. These are just temporal things and my children are eternal beings that still need guidance, love and support.

Many people didn't understand this and thought I was crazy to pass up such a great opportunity. I courageously told Craig that I could not take the full time position and thankfully he was able to put it in the job code that my position was being eliminated so I could qualify for a severance pay. They also put me on as a part time "floating secretary." This was truly a blessing in disguise. I was able to have many days off so I could spend time with my kids and not have to worry about going to a job every day. During this time was when God laid it on my heart to write this book.

As I continued to get my deepest needs met by God and embraced His love and my singleness with such a boldness and sureness, the kids started really thriving too. The peace came back in our home and they were more secure. Their relationship with God and with me grew to a whole new level.

Yes, through it all God really was and continues to be our father and our provider. I am now so thankful that I have the honor of living on my own. God continually shows Himself mighty on our behalf. Whenever any of my children have a need, it seems to always get met. In the seven years I have been a single mom, I have never made more than $25,000 (including child support) a year. Therefore, to actually have enough to pay the mortgage, food bill, water bill, power bill, and phone bill each month while living on our own, is baffling to me. We don't just live anyway we want to. I try my best to not spend money unwisely. We live a simple life and I make sure I pay my tithes and give back to God on a continual basis. Money is not just handed to us on a silver platter. We have to work hard, trust God and have faith to believe that He will continually provide for us.

However, the more I cry out to God, believing He will provide, the more His provisions overwhelm us.

> "Look at the birds of the air; they do not sow or reap or store away in barns, and yet your heavenly Father feeds them. Are you not much more valuable than they?" Matthew 6:26

> "I was young and now I am old, yet I have never seen the righteous forsaken or their children begging for bread." Psalms 37:25

He meets my kids' needs on a continual basis. Many times I cry out to God, asking Him to be a tangible father to my kids. I ask Him to teach, train, love, heal, minister to their hearts, provide, and protect them.

It is perplexing to me that my kids are actually thriving and even have special talents they are very good at! So many times I felt devastated that I could not give my kids dance lessons, music lessons, sports, or special academic classes to help them. In God's eyes it didn't matter because He was really teaching and training them and bringing out their gifts in amazing ways. What greater teacher than to have their own Creator teach them the very things they need to know so they can be that smooth stone who would one day help change their generation.

> "Come to Him [the risen Lord] as to a living Stone which men rejected and threw away, but which is choice and precious in the sight of God. You [believers], like living stones, are being built up into a spiritual house for a holy and dedicated priesthood, to offer spiritual sacrifices [that are] acceptable and pleasing to God through Jesus Christ." Peter 12:4–5

I have had people tell me how each one of my kids has blessed or encouraged them in some way or another. The only thing I can say is, "God is truly teaching them and I have to give Him the credit."

"I will instruct you and teach you in the way you should go; I will counsel you [who are willing to learn] with My eye upon you." Psalms 32:8

Children who are raised in a single parent home tend to have a stigma on them that they will be destined for failure. I am not accepting that label for my children; in fact I emphatically refuse it. My children have just as much potential as any other child in this world. I would like to encourage you, if you are a single mom reading this, do not accept that your child will amount to nothing because of the lack of a father in the home, even if the father is a "bad influence." Although this is a tragedy, as you continue to turn to God as your husband and father, He will make up for those losses in unbelievable ways.

My kids aren't at all perfect. Many times I have to mediate arguments, deal with sibling rivalry, and get upset when they don't do their chores or school work. At times, I lose my patience and handle things the wrong way. I have days of falling apart from utter exhaustion from having to wear the many hats of both mother and father. But again, God showers us with love and encouragement and continually gives me glimpses of my children's hearts. He shows me that each one has such a passion to live for Him and I don't ever have to worry.

Dalton wrote me a beautiful poem that made me burst into tears. I cried thanking God for my children who love and forgive me on a daily basis. So many times I beat myself up thinking I am a terrible mom but this poem confirms and reassures me of their great love for me.

MOM

When everything goes wrong, you are always singing a song.
You bring hope to my life even if there is strife.
You never let us down, you teach that God's in town.
And you always know what's right in God's sight.

Just wanted to let you know, Mom, that God loves you, and I think you're doing a great job. Love, Dalton (age twelve)

I really do not have any more fear. I have such a freedom and inner knowing that God is going to take care of us.

> "There is no fear in love [dread does not exist]. But perfect (complete, full-grown) love drives out fear, because fear involves [the expectation of divine] punishment, so the one who is afraid [of God's judgment] is not perfected in love [has not grown into a sufficient understanding of God's love]."- John 4:18

One night it was 11:00 and I had been asleep for a couple of hours. I kept hearing singing that woke me up. I followed the sound to Azaliah and Audrynn's bedroom and there they were, Adelynn 15, Dalton 13, Audrynn 10 and even Azaliah 7, singing the song "Amazing Grace." They were singing with such passion and desire. I just stood in awe of how well they harmonized and could sing together, glorifying God. Dalton and Adelynn were playing the guitars, they taught themselves how to play, with such clarity and ease. As I started recording it with my phone while listening to them sing such powerful words, tears of gratitude streamed down my face. My children stood there in front of me as a beautiful confirmation of God's undeserving and unmerited grace and love in my life. God really is a Good, Good Father to save such a wretch like me

Amazing grace! how sweet the sound,
That saved a wretch; like me!
I once was lost, but now am found,
Was blind, but now I see.[9]

---

9 Amazing Grace [Christian hymn published in 1779, with words written by the English poet and clergyman John Newton (1725–1807).]

CHAPTER 15
You Taught My Feet to Dance

As I ponder my life, I am astounded to see that God is definitely turning my mourning into dancing. My eyes are finally opened to the realization that when I turn to God and embrace my pain instead of turning to someone or something else just to numb my pain, is when Jesus' unconditional, relentless, pure love collides with my deepest human desperation, teaching my feet in the most beautiful, profound ways how to dance upon all my pain, despair, and disappointment.

> "You have turned my mourning into dancing for me; You have taken off my sackcloth and clothed me with joy, That my soul may sing praise to You and not be silent. O, Lord my God, I will give thanks to You forever." Psalms 30:11-12

The greatest representation of this dancing for me was when my dad and mom danced together. They loved it! They would do the jitterbug with such ease and motion. When we went to weddings and get-togethers where there was dancing, they usually stole the show. They even danced at home to Elvis and many other oldies. They flowed together as one. My dad would lead my mom with such a passionate love and a beautiful grace. And my mom followed with such anticipation and admiration.

Even a few days before my dad died, my parents danced a last dance together to celebrate their forty-eighth wedding anniversary. They were in Cape Cod, the same place they went on their honeymoon forty-eight years before. Here is my mom's take on it:

When our son, David, invited us to Cape Cod for the week of our forty-eighth wedding anniversary, we were so excited. We hadn't been there since our honeymoon, and we were so honored to be with him, his wife, Angelia, and his family.

We decided to bring the CD of our favorite "oldies" that had been given to us when we left Daryl's fiftieth class reunion the year before. We put the CD in to play "Sixteen Candles" for my granddaughter, Sidney Grace, who was celebrating her sixteenth birthday that day.

While the music was playing, Daryl surprisingly asked me to dance with him right there in the living room. With all of the family watching, he began to swing me around like when we were young—including the dip at the end! It was thrilling to me. Only God knew it would be our last dance together.

Just like my parents, Jesus and I are dancing, not a physical dance a couple would do, but a spiritual dance. Jesus leads and embraces me with such a pure, unconditional, powerful love that I want to eagerly follow His steps, one after the other. As I continue to move with Him, together we become synchronized and balanced, which ultimately creates a beautiful harmony.

Even if I mess up, Jesus quickly grabs me up and helps me get back into the rhythm of life with Him. Jesus really is daily teaching my feet to dance.

As I worship, obey and embrace God's love for me, the more our dance together magnifies, explodes and proclaims the awesomeness and holiness of God.

And this is why I wanted to write this book. I want to encourage you, my readers! Jesus longs to dance with you. You may

be going through the most difficult time of your life. You may
be feeling the most unbearable pain and have so much sadness
and chaos surrounding you that you can't even function. Death,
despair, hopelessness, discouragement, unforgiveness, bitterness,
regret, guilt, sickness, divorce, abuse or adultery might be beating
at your door.

But I am here to proclaim to you, loudly, confidently and
with the most clarity ever, *there is hope!*

I would like to sum up the key points of this book, praying
fervently that God will teach you, like He taught me, how to
dance!

The first step God taught me while dancing with Him is how
important it is to continually praise Him, worship Him and be
thankful at all times, even in the midst of your deepest sorrow.
Doing this brought the continual presence of God into my life,
which resulted in me receiving the greatest and most profound
revelation of His Word and the miraculous healing of our deepest
wounds.

The first step flowed with the next step, always walking in
obedience to God's Word. Obedience is the highest form of
worship. Obeying His commands and living a virtuous, pure
life, full of godly character, will result in God overwhelming you
with His amazing blessings. You will be free, safe, loved, and
protected when you obey.

"For the word of God is living and active and full of power
[making it operative, energizing, and effective]. It is sharper
than any two-edged sword, penetrating as far as the division
of the soul and spirit [the completeness of a person], and of
both joints and marrow [the deepest parts of our nature],
exposing and judging the very thoughts and intentions of the
heart." Hebrews 4:12

I really believe and know beyond any shadow of doubt that if
we had not applied God's Word to our lives, our health, healing
and restoration would never have happened. Don't feel guilty if
up until now you haven't been obedient. You may have chosen

to numb or escape your pain with a man, a woman, drugs, unforgiveness or bitterness. It is okay! God is an ever forgiving Father. He will embrace you with arms opened wide and help you get free from the bondage of sin. True freedom is a gift so many people have never opened. I don't ever again want to be a slave to my sin. Being daily weighted down with the chains of sin is profusely tormenting and only leads to death.

Last but not least, the third step God taught me is to daily receive and embrace the unconditional, unexplainable, life-changing, powerful love He has for you. Hearing that God loves you and knowing God loves you are two different things. You never want to live without knowing Jesus is real and alive and loves you so much that even if you were the only one left on the earth, He would have died for just you. This love causes you to live a fearless life!

God loves you so much. He always has and He always will. He loves everything about you, faults and all. He created you with such ingenuity and creativity. You are unequivocally the only you on this planet!

Do you know what the greatest thing is? When you truly grasp how much God intensely and uniquely loves you, you will have an insatiable desire to want to love Him back. These three steps that I share with you are not rules that you are forced to follow. Jesus will never make you dance with Him. However, the more you truly understand and know how much Jesus loves you, you will want to dance with Him. You will have such a desire to want to please Him that Obeying Him, Praising Him and Loving Him will just flow out of you. It will come from your heart. A great representation of this is when a woman gets married; would she just leave her husband at the altar or would she want to have a personal loving relationship with him, " dancing" with him every chance she got? You are the Bride of Christ! Jesus can truly be your husband . The best part is; He didn't propose to you on His knee, **He proposed to you on a cross** .

For your husband is your Maker ,The Lord of hosts is His name; And your Redeemer is the Holy One of Israel,Who is called the God of the whole earth." Isaiah 54:5 "

I would like to encourage you to allow other people to love you too, and surround yourself with a community of believers who will place courage in you and not let you have a "poor me" attitude.

Throughout this book I bravely bare my scars to you. I used my personal stories, woven with Scripture, to show you how God taught me in specific situations. Some of you might be saying, "Well, you were raised in church and had your parents and large community to fall back on and I don't have those privileges!" Don't believe this lie.

I am fervently praying that as you read my stories, God and His amazing presence and love will bring a miraculous healing, comfort and provision to you in your specific situation. As you cry out to God for help, I know he will surround you with real people that will help you. There is nothing I can do or say on my own that can change you and make you feel His love. So I cry out to Him, imploring Him to satisfy your deepest needs, praying that God's voice will be stronger than anything this world has to offer. I have seen Him move. I have seen Him turn tragedy to triumph. I have seen Him set feet to dance. Of course, your story will not be the same as mine and it doesn't matter because God doesn't favor anyone (Deuteronomy 10:17). God can be just as powerful in your life as He was in mine, if you just let Him. He longs to love you, have a personal relationship with you and teach you, so you can DANCE upon all your pain, all your suffering and all your disappointments.

Your tears will dry, your heart will mend,
10   *Your scars will heal and you will* Dance *again,*

---

10 © 2013 Integrity Music - CCLI #7002990. Matt Hooper

EPILOGUE

Looking back now, I can boldly say I am truly thankful for everything that I have had to go through. Yes, I could have easily chosen to numb my pain and wallow in my despair but then I would have tragically missed out on the beautiful dance of freedom, unexplainable blessings and most importantly, His powerful love and Presence.

Just recently Adelynn found this verse in Haggai 2:9 and shared it with me. After reading it, I know God is confirming the story of our lives in a beautiful, profound way.

"The latter glory of this house will be greater than the former,' says the Lord of hosts, 'and in this place I shall give [the ultimate] peace and prosperity,' declares the Lord of hosts."

Weston is now 20, Adelynn 16, Dalton 14, Audrynn 11 and Azaliah 8 and I have been a single mom for seven years. We haven't at all "arrived." We are still learning and growing every day. Our dance is not over; it is a daily choice to *dance* or to just sit it out.

I thank God on a continual basis that I have not had to deal with drugs, sex, abuse of alcohol or serious rebellion issues in any one of my kids. Jesus Christ is the reason that they are thriving and want to be everything God has called them to be.

Troy has moved to Ohio. Just in the past year, he has started really taking an active role in our children's lives. He spends time with them and values them. It has been hard at times but God is indeed restoring their relationship . We are walking in forgive - ness . Just today as I was finishing this final chapter, Troy texted me asking me if he could spend time with the kids, I told him yes . When Troy came to drop off the kids after spending time together I went outside and found they had put lawn chairs in a circle and started a little fire in a small grill we own. They all had their musical instruments playing songs together, laughing and singing.It was a beautiful sight because it was living proof that God was indeed answering our prayers and turning Troy 's heart back to his children.

> "He will turn the hearts of the fathers to their children, and the hearts of the children to their fathers [a reconciliation produced by repentance], so that I will not come and strike the land with a curse [of complete destruction]." Malachi 4:6

Who would have ever thought my dad's desire to carry me through my valley would be answered because his death caused me to turn completely and unashamedly to my Great Shepherd, my strength, my hope, my song, the one who *Taught My Feet To Dance.*

> *There's a time to weep and a time to laugh;*
> *A time to mourn and a time to* DANCE. *Ecclesiastes* 3:4

How He turned MY morning into Dancing - by Carol Myers:

I walked into my dentist's office to get a tooth worked on. Once the work was completed, Dr. Moor very timidly asked me my age. I told him I had just turned seventy. He then said the following to me, "I have a patient, who I have known for many years, recently ask me if I knew any 'godly widows in their sev- enties' he could meet. I told him I couldn't't think of anyone at the moment. Later your name came to me."

So I said to Dr. Moor, "Oh, I haven't even taken off my wedding band (it had been over two years since Daryl passed away). I will have to pray about it and let you know. How old is he?" He proceeded to pull up this man's dental chart which ended up being about ten inches from my face, with a picture of all of his teeth! I asked a few more questions and Dr. Moor continued to tell me the great love and respect he had for him and his family. Finally he said he wouldn't say anything to this man unless I contacted him to let him know it was okay.

When I left his office, I was shaken to the core. I began to pray immediately. I also asked some close Christian friends to join me in prayer. I had prayed a couple of times since I had lost Daryl that if I were to ever meet another man, God would bring him to me! I found out later that when Dr. Moor called Jim to give him my phone number, he said on the recording, "In my spirit, I can see the two of you together."

A little over a week later, after having prayed daily for this new scene in my life, I called Dr. Moor and told him he could give this man my phone number. An hour later the phone rang and Jim introduced himself to me. We talked for a while and he asked me to meet him for dinner. On May 1, 2014, we went out for dinner. It was a bit awkward, but we had a good connection. It was the first "date" either one of us had had in almost fifty years. I had been married forty-eight years and he had been married forty-seven years.

The morning of our first date, while praying about this encounter, I said to the Lord, "Father, if this is a man you are sending to be a part of my life, let it be like a candle lit and a fire burning!" On our second date, while walking into a restaurant, Jim touched my back to assist me through the door and the candle was lit! That night we found out we were born on the same date five years apart. Later, the fire began to burn. In fact, I couldn't eat or sleep for about six weeks. It was a matter of being apprehensive with a hint of excitement. We began to see that God had put us together. We prayed together over everything. We are very compatible and totally enjoyed being with each other. God works in mysterious ways, and His ways and thoughts are much higher than our ways and thoughts (Is. 55:8 &9). When we were going through the challenging time with all of us living together, I was crying out to the Lord daily for His intervention in our situation. One scripture I continually prayed was Psalm 27:13-14, "I would have despaired unless I had believed I would see the goodness of the Lord in the land of the living."

Only God Himself could have allowed Daryl's life to be taken in the perfect timing so that Erica and I both could experience Him turning our mourning into dancing.

ACKNOWLEDGEMENTS

I would like to first thank God for His unconditional love, never ending forgiveness and undeserving mercy and grace in my life.

My precious Dad, if only you could be here now. You would be shocked to see how God has transformed our lives and helped us climb out of our valley. Your words of wisdom still resonate within the walls of our home. I am so honored I had the privilege of being your daughter. I can't wait to see you again in heaven one day.

I don't know where I would be if it weren't for my mom's unstoppable love and prayers for me. She truly is the epitome of the Proverbs 31 woman. She is my mentor, my prayer partner, my greatest encourager, my truth teller and my best friend. Thank you for believing in me, Mom! I love you so very much!

There are not enough thank you's for my Five children. Your unwavering love and patience towards me is so undeserving at times. I love you so very much!

My special friend Gina has seen the good, the bad, and the ugly in my life, and I thank God for someone who never stops loving me and being there for me. Gina and I met fourteen years ago, and during those years we made many special memories together. We laughed and cried together, prayed together, went to church together, were pregnant together, homeschooled our children together, and even cleaned each other's house. She truly is a friend who sticks closer than a brother (Prov. 18:24). Thank you, Gina; I love you girl!

I want to thank my church, all the special friends God has surrounded me with and my pastors for their sacrificial love and encouragement. They have carried our burdens many times and have truly been "the church" in our lives. You have helped propel me out of my victim mentality and placed courage in me to keep on fighting. I will be forever grateful to you all!

I would like to thank a few special girl friends that were there for me many times. Thank you Heather for your love and beautiful friendship. The many times we had dinner and just talked was always at the perfect time. You are a true servant leader and I thank God on every remembrance of you. I am so grateful to you and Craig for all you have done to help me to see that my story is not over and I have a future and a hope. Thank you for loving my kids and babysitting them on so many occasions. We all love you and your family so much!

Thank you Gilda for taking my pictures for the back cover, helping me with my website and for your love and friendship over the years. You are an amazing single mom.

Thank you Kristen for allowing God to flow through you to minister to me in ways that were unbelievable. You were there for me in my most desperate times with just the right words.

Thank you Patti for your constant support and friendship during my most trying times. Even though you were going through the most difficult time of your life, you reached out of your pain and helped me in amazing ways. I am so glad that God brought that someone special into your life so you can live "happily ever after"

Thank you Rachel for believing in me as a tutor, friend and fellow sister in Christ. You and Tad's support over the years has helped us many times when we were at our lowest.

Thank you Susie, Tara and Coleen for letting my older kids come over to your homes, the many times that they did, so they could spend time with your kids.

Thank you Deena, for always being there and loving us during the times I didn't even know how to survive. You and Todd were an amazing source of strength to us all.

Thank you Elaine, Darlene and Ann. You have watched me grow up and have helped me more than words can say. Your letters of encouragement, your very wise counsel and how you love on my kids has placed courage in me hundreds of times. I will forever be grateful to you.

Thank you Nancy for being my prayer partner and helping a few of my children with their math. Your knowledge of the Bible and your love for God is so inspiring.

I would like to thank a dear couple Eric and Carissa who have faithfully sent me $100 per month for many years. This monthly check has helped us many times. May God continue to bless you and your boys above anything you could ever hope or imagine. We love you!

I feel like I have a band of brothers surrounding me at all times and I know that if I ever have a serious problem or concern, I can call on any one of you and you will help me. Do you know what an awesome comfort that is for a single mom? This is what true community looks like. I am beyond thankful for you! I pray God continues to bless your finances, health, wives, children, jobs and ministries above and beyond anything you could ever hope or imagine.

Thank you to all of my readers who sacrificially took the time to read my book and gave me your honest feedback. You all Rock!

I could not have written this book without the help of my author coach Kary Oberbrunner. When I had my first interview with him, he didn't see me as a single mom with five kids. He saw greatness in me even when I didn't see it myself. He gave me productive tools to help me write my story the best way possible. Most importantly, his heart was to ignite my soul so that I could ignite others.

ABOUT THE AUTHOR

Erica Marie Foster is a single mother to five beautiful children. Her story is powerful in the fact that even though she is raising her children on her own, God has specifically told her how important it is to daily look at her children as her calling and ministry and not as a distraction trying to steal another, better calling away from her. As long as she puts Him first and teaches her kids to know Him, then God promises her He will always provide for them. Erica has story after story of His amazing provision and stands in awe of it. Even though her kids have gone through deep sorrow, their intense love for God is a true testimony of His amazing provision in their lives. Her favorite quote is:

"Are the things you are living for worth Christ dying for?"

-Leonard Ravenhill

Erica has a passion to encouage and empower married or single mothers. Through her very transparent writing, speaking and coaching, she boldly and bravely shares her fierce love for Jesus and her children. She uses the Bible and gut-honest stories to help mothers live with faith, freedom and purity so that they will unashamedly embrace their calling to deeply love and raise their children to know God. Erica is a mother first, speaker coach and author. She is a member of the Igniting Souls tribe and Author Academy Elite led by Kary Oberbrunner. She was a pastor's wife for fifteen years and has counseled many women in all walks of life. In her free time she loves to write, sing, spend time with her family, play sports and be outside enjoying God's creation.

Contact Erica

Erica Foster
P.O. Box 126
Delaware, Ohio
43015

Email

ericamariefoster@gmail.com

Or visit her website at

www.ericamariefoster.com

You may also find her on Facebook

@ericamariefosterauthor

Made in the USA
Middletown, DE
07 August 2017